CRISIS TIME!

CRISIS TIME!

Love, Marriage, and the Male at Mid-Life

WILLIAM A. NOLEN, M.D.

DODD, MEAD & COMPANY
New York

Copyright © 1984 by William A. Nolen
Published by Dodd, Mead & Company, Inc.
79 Madison Avenue, New York, N.Y. 10016
Distributed in Canada by
McClelland and Stewart Limited, Toronto
Manufactured in the United States of America
Designed by Helen Winfield
FIRST EDITION

Library of Congress Cataloging in Publication Data

Nolen, William A., 1928-
Crisis time!
1. Men—Psychology.   2. Middle age—Psychological
aspects.   I. Title.
BF692.5.N65   1984   155.6'32   84-6116
ISBN 0-396-08404-4

To my wife, Joan,
for not tossing me out on my ear

Contents

CRISIS TIME!

Introduction

Every man, sometime between his thirtieth and sixtieth year (with the heaviest concentration between forty-five and fifty-five), goes through a mid-life crisis. "Not true," the reader may say. "I know a man of sixty who has never gone through a mid-life crisis." "Nonsense," is my answer. "Ask him. His breakdown—and the mid-life crisis *is* a breakdown—happened, but he managed to hide it from his friends, though not, I'll bet, from his wife. A mid-life crisis is an inevitable part of life."

The symptoms and signs aren't the same in all men. One man's problem may be mostly sexual, another's depression, but in most cases there is a combination of many problems, varying in duration and intensity. The one thing all male mid-life crises have in common is that they are extremely distressing, not only for the man but for those close to him; his co-workers, his employees, his friends, and his family. In fact, the one who often suffers as much or more than the man is his wife. (I might say, these days, "wife" or "significant other," but that gets awkward, so just assume, from this point on, that the word *wife* covers both situations.)

What is terribly frustrating for the man and those close to him is that the condition we call mid-life crisis is not clearly defined. It's not like pneumonia, or a broken leg, or a heart attack. There isn't any fever, there's nothing to be seen on X-ray, the electrocardiogram isn't diagnostic. It's very real—ask the man who is suffering through it—but it's not recognized by doctors as a disease. However, if we take the word *disease* (without ease) literally, few conditions fit the definition better than the mid-life crisis does.

Figures aren't available—no one can tell you the annual incidence of male mid-life crises—but, based on my study of the problem, I am willing to bet that more marriages and careers are annually crippled or destroyed by the male mid-life crisis (which I shall sometimes refer to simply as crisis) than by any other single entity. Men involved in a mid-life crisis flounder around, not recognized as needing help, until the condition simply wears out the man, his wife, his employer, employees, or associates. If there is one condition about which men and women need to know as much as possible, it is the male mid-life crisis.

Unfortunately, the man who is going through a mid-life crisis often isn't aware, at the time, that there is anything specific the matter with him. He feels "down," perhaps, and he may well wonder how he has managed to get his life so messed up, but he doesn't realize that he is actually in a crisis. The condition develops so insidiously that often those who are closest to him realize he has a problem long before he does. Without the advice and help of others he may not realize what has happened to him until the crisis is over, by which time he may well have made a shambles of his life.

Close friends or business associates may be the first ones to recognize that the man is not as he once was, that his behavior is out of character and self-destructive. But, if he has a wife, it is highly probable that she will be the first one to notice that he has changed. She is probably closer to him, both figuratively and actually, then anyone else, and she has probably known him long enough so that any change in his

life-style will quickly be obvious to her. (Whoever first becomes aware that a man is in a mid-life crisis will be doing
him a kindness by speaking out, gently of course, and either
offering him help or suggesting that he seek it somewhere.)

The wife who recognizes her husband's crisis problem early,
and deals with it promptly and correctly, has an excellent
chance of saving both her husband's life (figuratively and,
sometimes, actually) and their marriage. And, as we shall
see, if she can't save either him or their marriage she can at
least save herself.

I went through my own mid-life crisis a few years ago.
That, in fact, is what got me so interested in the condition.
I suppose it would be overdramatic to say that my mid-life
crisis almost cost me my life, but it wouldn't be much of an
exaggeration. Certainly, it almost cost me my wife, my family, and my profession. I hope I shall never again come as
close to disaster as I did then. When I was finally over my
mid-life crisis, I did some superficial research on the subject,
talked with a few other men who were going through similar
experiences, or had already done so, and suggested to my
editor at *McCall's* that an article on the subject might be of
interest to their readers. My editor agreed so I wrote a brief
piece on my experience (which *McCall's* published under the
title, "Why Men Go Crazy In Their Forties"). *Reader's Digest*
published a condensed version a few months later. After each
publication my mail became extremely heavy for several
weeks and the phone calls were almost as numerous. About
80 percent of the letters and calls were from women whose
husbands were going through similar crises. The other 20
percent were from the men themselves. In all cases what
they wanted was advice. The women wanted me to tell them
how to get their husbands through their crises and bring
them back to normal. "All I want is to have him be the
wonderful husband he once was," was a theme repeated again
and again. The husbands who called and wrote were, them-

selves, aware that they weren't "normal" any longer; they too wanted advice and help. In almost every case the wife, or husband, or both had already been to the family doctor (and sometimes to the minister and/or a marriage counselor) and the advice had generally been, "Don't worry about it. You'll get over it." Not much consolation for deeply troubled people.

I'd been writing for general circulation magazines for fifteen years, sometimes on controversial subjects, but the response to this article was at least twice as great as any I'd had to previous articles. For every person who writes to an author you can be certain there are hundreds of others who thought about writing and never got around to it, so I knew the article had struck a sensitive nerve. I found it frustrating to realize that, although I could describe the problem, I couldn't provide the solution. All around me men and women were suffering, marriages were breaking up, families were in turmoil, and I had no real advice to give those who called on me. Here, for example, is a letter typical of those I received:

Dear Dr. Nolen:

I read your article "Male Menopause: Myth or Mid-Life Reality?" in last month's *Reader's Digest* with great interest.

My husband and I were happily married for twenty-five years. (We have three beautiful daughters and four adorable grandchildren and we've always been *very* close.)

My husband was a minister of the gospel, a foreign missionary and a Christian Educator.

Four years ago, after going through a very discouraging and traumatic experience in a church split, he left the ministry weary, depressed, and very discouraged. He started drinking heavily and he stayed out to all hours of the night. When I'd ask where he'd been he'd say "none of your business."

We moved to Texas so that we could be close to our families. Immediately (within a month or two) he became involved with a girl eighteen years younger than himself and insisted on a divorce. I was, and still am, heartbroken because I love him dearly. She was a girl of very loose morals who has slept with numerous men. She also has two small children. I knew them both well enough to know it wouldn't last long. He has attempted to leave her and come back to me about six different times but she always lures him back! About a year ago he became involved with an old high school girl friend and has bounced back and forth between the two of them for the past year—still keeping in touch with me and asking that I don't give up on him.

He has completely changed life-styles, etc. and I *know* he's going through *mid-life crisis* (male menopause).

He has a master's degree in Guidance and Counseling so it's been impossible for me or his mother to get him to go for professional counseling or any kind of help. Actually, I don't know anyone in this area who specializes in helping men with this problem (Houston area). Do you? If you do, would you *please* send me their names, addresses, etc.

I love my husband so very much and will do anything within my power to help him. If he doesn't get help soon, I'm afraid he'll wind up a ruined man. (He is now *forty-eight*.) He's changed jobs about four times since this happened. He still *insists* on coming to help me with repairs, etc. around the house.

I will greatly appreciate any help or advice you can give me. I wish I knew someone to refer him to. I believe he'd go if you could suggest someone. He has read your article, too, at my request.

Thank you kindly for your time and attention.

Sincerely,

When people are in trouble, they don't want consolation, they want help. I could have cried for this woman, and the hundreds of others who wrote to me, but I couldn't help them.

And that's when I decided to write this book. It was obvious that at any one time there were probably tens of thousands of men going through mid-life crises, and an equal number of women who were trying to help them survive, intact. What could be done to ease their pain? Not just trite suggestions like, "Don't worry about it; you'll be better soon," but specific advice to help them overcome each of the many problems a mid-life crisis involves. I went back to my research—read all I could find in both the general and medical literature, and talked at length not only with men and women whose profession it was to help men in crisis, but with many more men who were going through or had been through crises. I also talked to the wives, friends, and associates of these men. I found, after almost three years of work, that there was, indeed, useful advice to be offered to men in crisis and their wives and friends. There wasn't any one answer that would fit every case, since men and their circumstances vary so greatly, but there were problems and patterns that appeared consistently and for these, answers could be found. Those are the answers that form much of the substance of this book.

But before we get to them, it seems appropriate to write first of my personal experience with the male mid-life crisis.

ONE

My Crisis

In 1978, shortly after my fiftieth birthday, my life began to fall apart. Let me start with some background.

My wife, Joan, was then forty-nine—she's fifteen months younger than I am—and we had been married since 1953. We have six children. Jimmy was born in 1954, Jody in 1955, Billy in 1956, Annie in 1958, Julius in 1959, and Mary in 1962. Between Julius and Mary, Joan had a couple of miscarriages. Two years after Mary, a seventh child, Christopher, was born, but he lived only a couple of hours. He died of a congenital anomaly: he had a diaphragm on only one side of his chest. Joan and I both interpreted his death as a sign that we'd had all the children the Lord meant us to have and that birth control would now be acceptable. (That is known as "rationalization.")

Since 1960 we had been living in Litchfield, Minnesota, a town of 5,000, seventy-five miles west of Minneapolis. It's a farming community, the county seat of Meeker County (pop. 18,000). The eighty-five-bed Meeker County Hospital is in Litchfield and I had been Chief of Surgery at the hospital ever since I had arrived in Litchfield. Some people said I was Chief of Surgery because I was the only trained surgeon in the county, and I suppose there was some truth in that.

1

Joan and I had both been born and raised in western Massachusetts. We had married in 1953, when I was an intern at Bellevue Hospital in New York. We had spent 1955–57 in Igloo, South Dakota, where the army had sent me to serve as a medical officer. In Igloo my co-worker was Don Dille, a G.P. from Litchfield, and Joan and I got along well with him and his family. In 1957, on our way back to New York from Igloo, we had visited Don in Litchfield and we liked the community. We kept in touch and in 1960, when I finished my surgical training, Joan and I decided to accept Don's invitation to join the Litchfield Clinic. It seemed to us that Litchfield might be a nice place to raise a family.

In 1978 I had a busy surgical practice; four of our six children were in college and I was in good health, having fully recovered from a double coronary artery bypass that had been done in 1975. I also had a busy career as a writer, an avocation that I had turned to in 1960 but which had become a second full-time career after the publication of *The Making of a Surgeon* in 1970. In 1978 I was working on another book, writing a monthly medical column for *McCall's*, free-lancing articles for other magazines, and doing occasional book reviews for the Minneapolis paper. I was a very busy person, but happy with both my work and my family. Joan had been very busy raising our family and she was just beginning to enjoy some leisure time now that five of the kids had gone off to college or to work. I thought she was reasonably happy, as was I, and she assures me that this was the case.

Until, as I've said, I began to fall apart in 1978.

It started with insomnia. I have always been a light sleeper. When the kids were babies I was usually the one who woke up when one of them whimpered. (On the nights I was home, that is; during most of the five Bellevue years I spent every other night and every other weekend at the hospital.) The first ring of a telephone always wakes me. Usually, however,

I could get back to sleep quickly. I think most doctors acquire that ability early in their training.

At fifty, however, I suddenly found that once I woke I had a difficult time getting back to sleep. I would lie, for what seemed like hours, worrying about all sorts of things: how I was going to pay tuitions; whether the patients I had operated on that day were going to be all right; whether I'd be able to come up with a decent idea for the *McCall's* column that was due. Often I'd wonder if we shouldn't get out of Litchfield. This had been a recurring consideration over the years and several times I had looked around for, and been offered, other professional opportunities. But always, usually with mixed emotions, we'd turned them down. Now I'd lie awake wondering if we hadn't made a mistake by not moving elsewhere years ago. At fifty, with a double coronary artery bypass, professional opportunities, even if I sought them out, were likely to be scarce. By 1978 the doctor shortage was all but nonexistent, and surgeons were a glut on the market. I'd finally drift off to sleep about 6:00 in the morning and, of course, I'd have to be up by 7:30 and in the operating room at 8:00.

I'm one of those people who decide whether or not they're tired by adding up the number of hours of sleep they've had. If I've had eight hours sleep, I'm not tired; if I've had seven I'm a bit tired; and if I've had only six I'm exhausted. This is nonsense, of course; at fifty most of us don't really need more than five or six hours of sleep a night. But if you think you should be tired you'll feel tired.

My answer to the insomnia problem was to drink before I went to bed. I've never been a teetotaler, but I usually drank in moderation. Once in a while I'd drink to excess. Everyone in Litchfield knew that; you don't keep drinking habits secret in a town of 5,000, particularly if you're a surgeon—but those occasions were rare. Now I started drinking fairly heavily almost every night.

The booze helped me to fall asleep, of course, but that hadn't really been my problem. My insomnia was the kind that struck in the early hours of the morning, two or three hours after I'd gone to sleep, and alcohol only makes that kind of insomnia worse. I had been waking up at about 4:00 A.M., but now I'd go to bed at 10:00, wake up at 2:00, and not only would I have difficulty getting back to sleep, but I'd feel physically ill from the liquor. After that had gone on for a couple of months I was, in fact, physically and emotionally exhausted. I had also started to change in other ways.

Racquetball, for example. All my life I had been physically active. I had even played ice hockey regularly with the men's team in town until I had my bypass operation in 1975 when I was forty-seven. I gave up hockey after my heart surgery, but I had continued to play vigorous tennis in the spring and summer and racquetball in the fall, winter, and spring. If I went without vigorous exercise for more than a couple of days I'd feel restless. Now I just didn't have the energy to play racquetball. Once in a while, if someone called me, I'd play, but I'd never take the initiative and try to arrange a game. Until I went into this slump I had played racquetball three or four times a week. Now I rarely played more than once a week, and sometimes not at all.

As far as sex was concerned, I became a nonparticipant. I have no intention of writing in any detail about my sex life—I've always felt that a writer who did that wasn't fair to his (or her) family—but I will say that in three months I went from an active, satisfying, full sex life to almost none at all. I wasn't impotent, but my libido was all but absent. Joan didn't mention it and neither did I, but we were both well aware that a radical change had occurred.

As far as my surgical practice was concerned, I carried on, but I became extremely apathetic about it. I had always enjoyed challenging cases—surgical problems that required a little extra ingenuity or dexterity—but now I much preferred relatively simple cases: hernias, appendectomies, even hemorrhoidectomies, to major cancer cases or complicated orthopedic problems. Like most surgeons, I've never particularly enjoyed the office part of my practice—surgeons like to be in the operating room—but now I'd hardly give an office patient any attention at all. If I had been financially able to quit, I probably would have done so. In retrospect, the fact that I couldn't quit was certainly one of the things that helped me.

My practice suffered. My associates sensed that I wasn't interested in operating, and patients felt I wasn't sufficiently concerned about their problems. Patients were referred elsewhere either by choice of the local G.P.s or because the patients requested referrals. My partners stood by me and kept me respectably busy, but not nearly as busy as I had once been.

The only child still at home was Mary, and she was so busy with high school activities that I don't think she really noticed any change in me. Joan did, of course, and she was concerned, but baffled. She didn't know what sort of line to take; should she be sympathetic or should she give me hell? Sometimes she took one approach, sometimes the other, but it didn't really matter; within six months of the time I started to fall apart I was living in my own little world. By that I mean the world people enter when they start taking drugs. We are a drug-obsessed society. In the United States, every year several million prescriptions are written for Valium alone. Millions of others are written for the other tranquilizers or analgesics that so many of us take to rid ourselves of pain, emotional or physical. When we take these medicines we leave the real world behind and escape the troubles that otherwise plague us. I used Valium and Quaalude to flee the pain of my mid-life crisis.

Insomnia and my general apathy are what got me started. When I'd get up at 7:30 to go and operate I'd feel exhausted, not so much from actual loss of sleep as from the thought that I wasn't sleeping enough. I'd also feel exhausted because I simply didn't want to get out of bed. I had no desire to get up and get out and do things. Consequently, on the days when I didn't have to operate I'd take a couple of five-milligram Valiums and go back to bed until 10:00 or 11:00 in the morning. When I'd get up, I'd go to the hospital and make rounds. Not once—even when I was in the depths of my crisis—did I ever go into the operating room under the influence of drugs or alcohol. Twice I postponed cases because I was uncertain of my control. Never did I pick up a scalpel when my mind and hand were under less than full control.

By then, that wasn't all I was taking. Since I was drinking quite a lot every evening, there were, naturally, mornings when I woke with a hangover. Almost invariably this would occur on Sunday morning, though once in a while it happened on a Saturday. Anyone who has ever had a hangover knows that if there is one thing a person with a hangover would like to do it's to go back to sleep for about three hours. And if there is one thing a person with a hangover cannot do, it is get back to sleep. It just can't be done—without drugs, that is.

I discovered that there was one way I could get back to sleep on hangover Sunday mornings: I'd take 30 milligrams of Valium. That worked well the first couple of times, and I'd wake up a second time at about noon on Sunday feeling refreshed. But after the first couple of times 30 milligrams of Valium wouldn't do it so, rather than increase my Valium dose, I'd add 150 milligrams of Quaalude. When I grew tolerant to that, I raised the dose to 300 milligrams. When that no longer did it I worked out a new plan. I'd get up about 7:30 Sunday morning with my hangover and take out a bottle of vodka and a quart of grapefruit juice. Then I'd unplug the telephone and sit in my comfortable chair in the living room and, over the next two or three hours, I'd have four or five nice tall glasses of vodka and grapefruit juice. After the first hour I'd swallow 30 milligrams of Valium and after the second hour I'd take 300 milligrams of Quaalude. Usually by then I would have one hell of a buzz on and, often, I'd plug the phone in and call a few friends I hadn't talked to for several years. I'm sure, looking back, that they must have been intrigued—to put it kindly—by my undoubtedly incoherent conversation. About 11:00, full of pills and booze, I'd go back to bed and sleep until 2:00 or 3:00 in the afternoon. Such was my tolerance by then that I'd actually feel very well by the time I finally got up. Of course, having slept away so much of the day, the only way I'd be able to get to sleep at night was to have a few more drinks and a pill or eight.

When Joan would get up on Sunday morning, to find me sitting in my chair, reading a book and drinking, she would plead with me just to go back to bed. I'd explain that I couldn't sleep, that I needed just a couple of drinks, and she'd try, unsuccessfully, to talk me out of it. Even after plugging the phone back in, she would make sure that on those mornings no phone calls ever reached me; I don't think I'd have been crazy enough to visit a patient, but who knows? The opportunity, thank God, never presented itself. Those Sundays, Joan tells me now, were the worst days of our life together.

In October of that year (my birthday had been in March) I flew to North Dakota to speak at a medical meeting. I was fine at the time I spoke, but at a dinner party afterward I behaved like an absolute idiot. I drank martinis—always destructive, even taken alone—but combined with the Valium, which I now took in ten-milligram doses whenever I felt the need to relax, I would go completely out of control. One of the side effects of Valium is that it interferes with your sense of balance and it was now routine for me to start stumbling whenever I'd had a couple of drinks. I'd trip over chairs or even over my own feet. More than once I fell flat on the floor, where I would lie contentedly for quite a while, if I were home or at some other place where no one would disturb me.

Later that same month I flew to Chicago to the annual meeting of the American College of Surgeons. I had an assignment from *Esquire* to write a piece on the convention, explaining to a lay audience what the purpose of the convention was and what went on both at the scientific meetings and during the parties that are a routine part of the convention. It was to be a behind-the-scenes report of the college's annual meeting.

I arrived at my convention hotel at 10:00 on Sunday morning nursing a raging hangover. I wanted a beer very badly and was shocked to find the bars in Chicago didn't open until noon. As the clock struck that hour I plopped myself down at the hotel bar and ordered a nice cold Heineken. I had three or four, followed by a sandwich, and then went back to my room to sleep. That evening, under reasonably good control, I talked with some old friends whom I bumped into in the hotel lobby, had a couple of drinks, took a few pills, and went to bed. The next morning I was fine and I stayed under control for three days. Then, on Wednesday afternoon, I met one of the fellows who had been a very close friend and co-worker when we were interns on the Cornell Surgical Division at Bellevue. I'd seen a couple of other fellows at the convention who had been at Bellevue and so had he. I suggested we all get together in my room—a small suite—about 6:30 that evening. About a dozen of us, some with wives, made the meeting, and after several drinks we went out to dinner. By now my tolerance for alcohol was very low and by the time we got to the restaurant I was, to put it plainly, drunk. Not funny drunk but sloppy drunk. I behaved boorishly through the entire meal. I've always wanted to apologize to my friends for my boorish behavior that evening, but I haven't seen them since that night. If they're avoiding me, I can't say that I blame them.

Thursday morning I woke up with an unmerciful hangover. I used my home treatment—several drinks and half a dozen pills taken between 8:00 and 9:00 A.M. I fell asleep again until 11:00. I got up, had two more drinks, packed, and flew back to Minneapolis, where I was to meet Joan at a motel near the airport. I was flying first class and, on the one-hour flight from Chicago to Minneapolis, I had at least four more drinks. The stewardess apparently recognized me (I appear on television with some frequency in Minneapolis) and, despite my protestations, she had a porter with a wheelchair meet me when the plane landed. He wheeled me to the front entrance of the airport where I caught a cab for the ten-minute ride to the motel. When Joan opened the door to our room, in response to my knock, I could actually see her slump. "Oh, Bill," she said, almost crying, "what are we going to do?"

That moment was, in retrospect, the nadir of what we now look back upon as my mid-life crisis. I realized then that I couldn't go on like this and neither could Joan. Over the next couple of months I fiddled around, trying to cut back on both pills and drinking, but wasn't successful. Finally, in January, ten months after I'd started my downward slide, I went through one night that actually scared me. Joan and I were in Minneapolis, where I was to appear on a television show at 9:00 the next morning. I had a few drinks, took 300 milligrams of Quaalude and 30 milligrams of Valium, and went to bed and to sleep. Two hours later I was wide awake, so I took an additional 600 milligrams of Quaalude. Two hours after that, wide awake again, I took another 600 milligrams. That total dose would have killed most people, but it hardly affected me. The next morning, after the television show (which Joan watched; amazingly, she said I looked and spoke very well),

I went back to my room, took another 30 milligrams of Valium, and slept for an hour. When I woke up I went over, mentally, all the medicine and booze I'd taken in the last twenty-four hours and came to the conclusion that I had had it. I just couldn't go on this way, not without killing myself. Joan agreed. "I can't take it either, Bill," she said. "You're miserable and you're making life miserable for everyone close to you. You've got to do something." I picked up the phone, called the office of the internist who had been my doctor ever since I moved to Litchfield, and said, "Joe, I'm in trouble, I need help." I told him what my life was like, telling him honestly about the pills I'd been taking, and when I was finished he said, "Right, you do need help. I'm off this afternoon, but I'd better see you. Can you and Joan meet me for lunch?" I said we could. An hour later I started the long haul back to what passes for normal.

II

Before I get to the meeting with my internist, let me explain something. At that point I admittedly had a drug problem of some magnitude, but there were other, deeper underlying causes for that problem.

My crisis seemed to me to start with insomnia, but why, at the age of fifty, did I suddenly develop insomnia? There were several reasons.

First, I was not, physically, the person I had been ten or even five years earlier. Humans tend to peak, physically, at about twenty-five; that's when they're at their best. After twenty-five, the general tendency is to slip, physically, downhill. Eating nutritious food; avoiding tobacco and alcohol; keeping one's weight at acceptable levels; exercising regularly; sleeping regularly; avoiding stress—all these things will help to keep one in good physical shape for a long time, but there's nothing that will stop the aging process. No matter how well we take care of ourselves, muscle tone decreases, skin begins to sag, stamina declines as we get older. I was, at fifty, well past my physical peak.

Certainly, I hadn't taken care of myself as well as I should have, but few of us do. I'd exercised regularly and kept my weight at a reasonable level, but the one thing I had not done—could not do—was avoid stress. None of us can avoid stress entirely—that's not the nature of life in the United States in the 1980s—but in many jobs, depending on one's responsibilities, stress can be overwhelming. My job fell into that category.

I was, after all, the only trained general surgeon in Meeker County. For almost twenty years I had been on call twenty-four hours a day every day I was in Litchfield, which was almost every day; I spent only about thirty days a year out of town. Admittedly my phone didn't ring as often as did those of the G.P.s, but the G.P.s always knew that they could refer patients to each other or to me. I couldn't refer patients to anyone, not without sending them to another city, and the closest city with a general surgeon was thirty-five miles away. If a man came in with a perforated ulcer, a woman with a ruptured ectopic pregnancy, a child with a ruptured spleen, I had to go immediately to the hospital and start operating. If I didn't do it, no one else could, and there was a good possibility that the patient would die. Mine was a hell of a stressful way to live.

I thought I had gotten used to it, but of course I hadn't; no one can possibly get used to being on call all the time, day and night, to take care of patients in critical condition. I had always jumped a little when the telephone rang. I had a special line in our home, with a special ring for the children, so that I wouldn't jump quite as often as I otherwise would have.

Over the last two years before my crisis I knew I was jumping more than ever at the sound of the phone. To say that I hated its ring would be a gigantic understatement. Not only the aging process but the stress of my job was taking a physical toll.

A psychological one, too. I was short-tempered with Joan, my children, my friends, in part, I'm sure, because I couldn't reasonably yell at the telephone. I felt trapped. On the one hand, I considered trying to get another surgeon to come to Litchfield; on the other, I was afraid that a second surgeon might cut into my practice significantly and reduce my income substantially. There's a saying, "Money is like sex; only too much is enough." I felt that way. In 1978 I still had four children to get through college. I made enough money so that my children weren't eligible for scholarships, but not enough so that I could pay tuitions, board, and room and still live in reasonable comfort; not unless I kept my income where it was. I knew we needed another surgeon in town, not just for my sake but for that of Litchfield as well, but I didn't dare go out and recruit one. I was torn between wanting another surgeon, to give me some relief, and not wanting one for fear of what he might do to my income.

Another thing that, I suppose, had tipped me into this crisis, was my fiftieth birthday. I later learned that birthdays—particularly the fiftieth—tend to precipitate mid-life crises. It's common for a patient to go into a depression after a heart attack or a bypass operation, but that hadn't happened to me. I think I missed that depression because I had faith in the bypass and figured it had at least temporarily preserved me from a premature death. But my fiftieth birthday was a significant landmark: my father had died, at fifty-eight, of heart disease; genetically I seemed to be like my father, and I figured, I probably had just eight years left. When I'd lie awake at night I'd think about all the things I'd like to do and the places I'd like to go and I'd realize that, in all probability, I wouldn't do these things and visit these places. At fifty, with a double bypass, I wasn't the world's best bet in a longevity race. Too late now to take three years off and study law; too late now to set up a Park Avenue practice and lead the lush life in Manhattan; too late now to move to Big Sur and become a California hippy. At fifty my options were rapidly narrowing, and I hated to see that happening.

It wasn't just my age and my health that had me trapped; after all, the bypass had worked very well and who knew— maybe I was good for another twenty years? Even if that were true, how could I possibly give up what I had and start over? I had too many obligations. I felt I owed my kids their education; they were good kids, good students, and I wanted them to have whatever education they wanted. It wouldn't be fair to pull the financial rug out from under them just because I was restless.

Nor did I think it would be fair to Joan. Raising six children is no easy job. Now, with only Mary at home, she could play golf or go cross-country skiing when she wanted to; she didn't have to feed eight people every evening; she could play bridge with her friends. She would have been perfectly happy if, in 1960, we had never left New England; in fact, she would have preferred to stay there, where we had friends and relatives. She accepted Minnesota only because she thought it would be a place I'd like to practice. Now, however, she was used to Litchfield. She liked her life. Because I was restless, was it fair to ask her to move? I didn't think so. I haven't any doubt she would have moved, if she thought it would help me, but it wasn't something she wanted to do. We'd been in Litchfield almost twenty years. We had roots. It was our home.

Now that I think back on that period, it's little wonder that, with all those things on my mind, I had insomnia. Nor is it strange that my libido had diminished. Nor is it surprising that I turned to booze and pills. Stupid, yes, but not surprising. I was in a mid-life crisis of mammoth proportions.

III

Now to our meeting with the internist. We met Joe at 12:45 at a restaurant on the west side of Minneapolis. The first thing he said, once we were seated at a table tucked in a corner, was "You look a lot healthier than I thought you would."

"I know," I said. "In fact I did a television show this morning and I thought it went very well. So did Joan."

"Really?" Joe asked Joan.

"Yes," Joan said. "I'm more surprised than you are. I don't know how he does it."

We ordered, and while we were waiting for our food Joe said, "Why don't you tell me all about it, from the beginning."

So I did. I talked right through lunch and coffee, beginning with my insomnia, my apathy toward surgery, my lack of interest in exercise and sex, and my problems with alcohol and pills. When I wasn't quite certain of the sequence, I'd ask Joan and she invariably remembered it all well; in fact, in excruciating, painful detail.

When I was finished, Joe said, "What a change! I remember just a couple of years ago how gung-ho you were about sports. Entering tournaments and all that business."

"I remember," I said. "Lately, I just haven't been able to get myself fired up to play."

"You're going to have to force yourself," Joe said. "Sitting around is the worst thing you can do."

He hesitated for a minute and then he said, "Have you ever thought that you're probably menopausal?"

"Menopausal?" I asked.

"Exactly," he said. "I'm sure that's what's wrong. I know some doctors don't like to use that term for males, but I've always thought it was appropriate. Hell, women aren't the only ones who go through a 'change of life.' The difference between the change of life in men and women is that in a woman there's something physical to mark the change; she stops menstruating. In a man, the onset is more subtle. But the physical and psychological changes are just as marked. I'm sure that's what's happening to you.

"Heck," Joe continued, "it happened to me three years ago when I was fifty. I've always been one of those guys who get up and get going early. I rarely stayed in bed after 6:00 A.M. and I was usually making rounds at the hospital by 6:45. All of a sudden I found myself lying in bed for an hour after the alarm went off. Just had no interest in getting moving. Phyllis wondered if something was wrong. It was February—a really cold, snowy month—and she thought the weather might be getting me down, so she suggested that maybe I needed a break. We took a week's vacation in Florida. As usual I brought along a pile of journals that had accumulated over the previous few months, thinking I'd catch up on my reading, but I found that my attention span was all but nonexistent. I'd read the first page of an article and when I'd turn to the second page I'd find I couldn't even remember what the subject was. Mostly all I did during the entire week was sleep— no swimming, no scuba diving, no fishing, no nothing. It wasn't much of a vacation.

"To make a long story short, let me just say that when I came back to Minneapolis I decided I needed to change the way I practiced medicine. I was just about burned out. I didn't need as much income as I'd been earning, now that the kids were out of school, so I stopped going to the office every day. Now I go three times a week. The other two days, and most weekends, I make rounds, and see my own patients if emergencies come up, but Phyllis and I have more time to ourselves. Oddly, my income hasn't dropped appreciably. I'm more relaxed, spend more time with every patient, and although I've raised my fees some, patients don't seem to mind. I guess my menopause was affecting the way I practiced, though I didn't realize it at the time.

"But that's enough about me. I just didn't want you to think a menopause wasn't a manly condition. If it weren't, I certainly wouldn't have had it." We both laughed.

Then we got down to business. "Whether we call it menopause or mid-life crisis, Bill, it's gotten you into trouble. The immediate problem is the fact that you're hooked on booze and pills. No sense in pretending otherwise. You've got a bad habit. All that Valium and Quaalude! I don't know how you can walk a straight line. The first thing you've got to decide is whether you want to go some place to get unhooked. Don't worry about word getting around; it won't. These places are very discreet. You know Charlie Thomas, the urologist? He got hooked on Valium and booze two years ago, went to Saint Agatha's and got off the stuff, and no one ever knew." Joe didn't even smile. To this day I don't think he realized it was a contradiction in terms for him to mention Thomas as an example of how no one ever heard about hospitalizations for drugs or booze.

I said I didn't want to go anywhere. "I'm sure I can beat it on my own," I said. Joe was from Minneapolis, a place big enough so that maybe a doctor could get away with being hospitalized for alcoholism. In Litchfield word would have gotten around in twenty-four hours. I didn't know how it would set in our conservative little town, and I didn't want to find out.

Joe shook his head. "Maybe, Bill, but I doubt it. You have a heavy habit. But if you want to try it, that's up to you. I'll tell you what you have to do."

First, he insisted that I quit cold turkey. Absolutely no more Valium, Quaalude, or alcohol. None at all. "It will be tough," he said, "but it's the only way to go. You'll have a terrible time sleeping for a while, but you must live through it."

"How long?" I asked. "Two or three days? I'd expect the Valium to be out of my system by then."

"More like three or four weeks," Joe said. "You've been on a lot of this stuff for a long time. Your sleep patterns are all deranged. It's going to take time for them to come back to normal. You're going to have a tough time. To be honest, I doubt very much that you'll make it without help. Call me if you change your mind.

"As far as exercise is concerned, you've got to push yourself. Make yourself call friends and arrange matches. The best thing you can do is get yourself physically exhausted. It will help you sleep.

"Apparently you've been handling your practice all right. Don't push it, but don't take time off either. You need the distraction. Hanging around with nothing to do would be the worst thing you could do to yourself.

"As far as sex is concerned, don't worry about it. When you get off the drugs and the alcohol and get back to a physical life, your libido will come back. You're not concerned, are you, Joan?"

"Not at all," Joan said. "Sex is the least of my worries. I just want him well again."

"You'll have other problems," Joe said, "and you'll solve them. Not with pills though; they're out. Just keep going. And call if you need help."

I thanked Joe, as did Joan. We were both relieved to have finally talked to someone about my deterioration. We drove back to the Minneapolis Athletic Club, where we were planning to spend the next two days; we were on a mini-vacation. "No matter what Joe says," I said, "I think that the first couple of days will be the worst. Once that stuff is out of my system I ought to begin to feel better."

Little did I know, and it's just as well. I took a nap as soon
as we got back to the club, and I wondered if Joe had been
right. I had no trouble dozing off for an hour.

That night I found out just how right he was. I went to
bed at 10:30 but at midnight I was still lying awake. I got
up, turned on a light, and sat and read for an hour. I had
trouble concentrating but managed to follow the plot line as
long as I read slowly. At 1:00 A.M. I went back to bed, apparently dozed off about 3:00, and was awake again at 4:00.
I lay in bed until 6:30, then got up, took a shower, and turned
the television on low. I watched the "Today Show" until Joan
woke at 8:00.

For the next six weeks my life, to put it simply, was sheer
hell. I may have slept a couple of hours a night (I know people
tend to underestimate the time they're asleep) but I really
don't think so. Most nights I don't think I slept at all. I'd go
to bed for a couple of hours, get up and read for a couple of
hours, and go back to bed for another couple of hours. I
figured that if I were lying down at least I was getting some
rest.

Two or three times a night cold shivers would pass through
my body. It was as if my muscles were going through waves
of contractions. They were like cramps. And often, after such
a wave, my pajamas would be wringing wet.

The waves didn't come just at night. Often I'd get to the
hospital at 7:45 in the morning, put on a scrub suit, and by
the time I had reached the scrub sink my scrub suit would
be soaked with perspiration. "Gee, you're sweating a lot,"
Chuck, our anesthetist, said on several occasions. "Yeah,"
I'd say, "maybe I'm getting the flu."

Three or four times a week I'd play racquetball. My game
was terrible—I think it was a combination of exhaustion and
nerves—but I played hard, hoping to get tired enough to
sleep. I can't honestly say it helped.

But I didn't drink and I didn't take pills. Al Nelson is one of the friends with whom I often played racquetball. Usually, after a game, we'd stop and have a couple of beers. Now I'd either have a Fresca or I'd make an excuse and just go home. I'd say I was trying to lose weight.

About two weeks after I'd quit all pills and alcohol, I got panicky. I wondered if I'd ever again have a decent night's sleep. Not wanting to call Joe, I decided instead to phone my cardiologist, back in Boston. Apologetically, I told him about my problem. "It doesn't sound too serious to me, Bill," he said. "You developed some bad habits and you have to get over them. You will. I know what that sleep problem is like; it's like sex. The more you want to, the more you can't, the more you want to. It may take a while longer but eventually your sleep pattern will get back to normal."

"Eventually" proved to be about four months. The change was so gradual I hardly noticed it. Two hours sleep once a night became two hours twice a night. Then I'd go three hours without waking. Suddenly I realized I was sleeping almost seven hours. I'd wake up once or twice a night, but that was just to go to the bathroom. I was over the insomnia.

The sweating ended about the same time. Once in a great while I'd still wake up with one of those horrible waves sweeping over me and I'd be wringing wet when it passed. If you think it sounds like a hot flash, let me assure you that I noticed the parallel, too. The only difference of which I'm aware was that I had excruciating muscle cramps with the perspiration. Since Valium is widely promoted as a muscle relaxant I theorize (admittedly, I can't prove this) that my muscle spasms were probably a reaction of my body to the fact that there was no longer any Valium circulating in my blood.

Gradually, my life returned to normal. I once again became a competitive racquetball player and enjoyed exercising. I had been unable to concentrate well when reading during the previous six months, but slowly my concentration returned. (It was one of the things that had bothered me most during my slump; I'm an avid reader, and not being able to concentrate was very painful.)

Strangely, even when I was going through the worst part of my withdrawal period, I was still able to do the appropriate research and then sit down and write whatever articles were due. Even the piece I wrote for *Esquire*—much of the data for which (as I've mentioned) was collected when I was near the bottom of the barrel, psychologically speaking— was published as a long piece with very little editing. I suppose that some parts of the brain aren't affected by whatever chemical changes produce the male mid-life crises.

Often, in the eight years that had elapsed since *The Making of a Surgeon* had been published in 1970, I had wondered if I might not be happier if I gave up my surgical practice and devoted all my time to writing. There were four reasons why I had decided to stay in both professions. Even now, as I worked my way through my mid-life crisis and considered as an option dropping one profession, my four reasons for not doing so still seemed valid.

The first reason was a financial one. I had earned quite a bit of money with my first three books *(The Making of a Surgeon, A Surgeon's World,* and *Healing: A Doctor in Search of a Miracle),* but I had also learned that the writing profession was a financially precarious one. Whenever I began a new book, or even an article, I couldn't predict how readable it would be or how well (or even if) it would sell. What if I suddenly ran out of ideas for books or articles? That had happened to a lot of writers, as I well knew. I needed a reliable source of income to support my family. I knew that if I took out a gall bladder or an appendix I'd be paid, and paid reasonably well. I couldn't give up that financial security. I didn't have the sort of temperament that would let me live a comfortable life without a guaranteed income. I think I'd have had an ulcer or a heart attack in a very few months if I gave up the financial security that my surgical practice offered.

The second reason I didn't want to give up my surgical practice was that I still enjoyed it. It's very satisfying to be able to cure a patient of a cancer of the colon, or appendicitis, or chronic gall bladder disease. I think the surgical specialties attract so many young residents because they offer instant gratification that the medical specialties can't match. I wished that I could control my practice to a greater degree—I would have been delighted if I could have given up all night calls and emergency cases—but that wasn't possible in Litchfield. Faced with the choice of continuing with my entire practice load or giving it all up, I chose the former.

The third reason I had for not giving up my practice was the fact that it gave me something to write about. No one sees more real life drama than a surgeon. My ideas for articles and books came from my practice. I was afraid that if I gave up surgery I'd run out of ideas for books and articles very quickly.

The fourth and final reason for continuing my practice was that it gave me an authority I would otherwise have lacked in the writing profession. As a person who was actually in the operating room, operating on patients, my opinions on medical matters were based, in part, on personal experience. I don't think readers would have accepted me as an authority as readily, despite my M.D. degrees, if I had been on the sidelines, working only as a reporter.

What about the alternative possibility: giving up writing and just practicing surgery? Wouldn't that have given me more free time, time to relax?

Certainly, but at a price I wasn't willing to pay. Doctor Samuel Johnson is often quoted as having said, "Only a fool writes for anything but money," but that isn't true. Certainly, and I suppose this was Doctor Johnson's point, writing is difficult. As someone else has said, "No one likes to write, but everyone likes to have written." It takes tremendous self-discipline to be a professional writer. But I wasn't writing just for the money.

What I really wanted when I began to write, and what I still want, is recognition. I could achieve local recognition because of my surgical skills while living and practicing in Litchfield, but I certainly wasn't going to achieve national or even statewide recognition. That depends on research or surgical ventures which require the equipment and supporting staff available only at major surgical centers. If I wanted recognition, and I did, it would have to come from something other than surgery. I chose to try to achieve it through writing.

Should I be ashamed of this? I don't think so. It's a perfectly natural desire. I remember well how the critics attacked Norman Podhoretz, the editor of *Commentary*, when he admitted, in his book *Making It*, that what he was after, when he entered the literary world, was recognition. He wanted to "make it." I remember the devastating article Rust Hills wrote in *Esquire;* it was called "Norman Podhoretz's Dirty Little Secret." But if the truth were known I think we'd discover that Podhoretz's dirty little secret (his desire for recognition) is one that most of us share.

In fact, for some men, one of the precipitating factors of the mid-life crisis may be the desire for recognition. They have become more or less acutely aware of their mortality—there aren't all that many years left—and when they die who will remember them? If they have received some sort of recognition during their life—whether for a painting, a poem or a book, or even a trophy awarded for winning the Class B tennis doubles championship of 1983 at their local country club, there will be something around to remind people that they once existed. Not for long, probably, but at least for a while.

If a man has children, that will give him another sort of transient immortality (a contradiction in terms, I realize) and it's the sort of immortality many of us achieve. But I have the feeling that mothers get more of a sense of immortality from children than do fathers. Eleanor Roosevelt, when asked near the end of her life what she considered her greatest accomplishment, answered, "My children." I don't know if anyone ever asked F.D.R. that question, but it's very unlikely he would have given the same answer.

So giving up writing was not an option I seriously considered. I had come to depend on my writing income, unpredictable as it was, to help significantly in supporting my family; and I still enjoyed the recognition that writing brought. As long as I thought I had something worth writing about, I intended to do as good a job of it as I could. A surgeon enjoys a pleasant sense of achievement when he has just performed a successful operation. An author gets a similar gratification when he writes what he considers a worthwhile article, story, or book. I was lucky enough to occasionally enjoy both of these feelings and I had no desire to give either one up.

Several times during the fifteen months of my crisis, before, during, and after my drug problem, I felt like chucking everything I was doing and moving on to a different life. I had wondered if I could get a job teaching English in a prep school; the security of the life appealed very strongly to me. I considered trying to enter the world of administrative medicine, where I wouldn't have to deal with the life-and-death crises that are part of the life of every practicing surgeon. I even considered changing careers entirely—perhaps selling off what assets I had and opening a restaurant.

I am thankful that Joan was around to discuss these possibilities with me. She was always gentle, never saying, "That's the craziest thing I've ever heard of," though I'm certain that at times that is exactly what she thought. Instead she'd say, "Well, if you really want to teach in a prep school, you'll have to get used to a lot less money. And it will be funny, now that we're just getting the last of the children out of the house, to start living again surrounded by hundreds of teen-agers." I'd think about that for a while and then, without saying anything more, let the idea drop.

As far as administrative medicine was concerned, Joan said, "That should be interesting. But don't administrators have to go to quite a few meetings? I know how you hate to go to the hospital staff meeting, and that's only once a month. Don't you think you'd kind of dislike having several meetings every week?" I argued that I could get used to it, but after thinking it over for about ten days I realized that life as an administrator, for someone with a temperament like mine, would be a living hell.

Joan disposed of the restaurant business quite deftly. "That sounds like fun," she said, "in fact I've always wanted to be a hostess in a restaurant. And you shouldn't have any diffi-culty finding one to buy. There always seem to be plenty for sale. Even places like Charlie's and the Black Angus that seem to be doing so well go under. Let's remember to check the classified ads this Sunday. It seems to me there's always at least one page with nothing but restaurants for sale." Even in my obtuse state the message got through to me. Eventu-ally, I decided I ought to think about it a little longer before I actually bought a restaurant.

When my crisis was all over, however, I did make some changes in my life. I decided, and Joan agreed, that we were going to get out of Litchfield at least once every two weeks. For nineteen years I had been on call every day and night that I had been in Litchfield. But I felt, now, that I couldn't take that kind of stress anymore. Since I couldn't avoid it in town, I had to get out of town. We did.

I also learned to unplug the telephone for an hour or so every noon. The nurses and secretaries at my office knew where I was; if there were any grave, surgical emergencies they could run over to my home (our home is only two doors away from the Clinic) and get me. If I was out at our lake cabin they could call one of my neighbors. But they wouldn't do either of these things unless it was truly an emergency situation. Otherwise, I had an hour every day free from the telephone.

After three months off all alcohol and pills I had begun to allow myself a couple of drinks in the evening. This I continued to do. No more pills—none at all—but I enjoy a couple of drinks in the evening and I didn't feel they did me any harm. Joan agreed.

As Joe had predicted, once I was off the pills and back to exercise my libido returned. True, I wasn't the stud that I once was, but very few men of fifty-two have as great a sex drive as they had at forty-two. They may feel as if they should have an undiminished sex drive, but the years take a toll. Joan and I were back to what I think we both considered a very satisfactory sex life.

The one thing that had never occurred to me, though it's a major concern for some men in mid-life crises, was the thought of leaving Joan and attaching myself to some other woman. There have been times when people in Litchfield have suspected that I "had something going" with one woman or another from Litchfield. And I'm certain that I've upset Joan many times during the years we've been married. But I have never wanted anyone else to be my wife. I love her— always have—and I guess I always will. With some exceptions—and the fifteen months of my crisis were certainly a major one—we've had a wonderful, full life together.

I seem to have suggested that my crisis came to an abrupt halt at the end of the fifteen months. That isn't true. Over the following six or eight months I'd have occasional slumps, days when I had to force myself to get up and get going. Sometimes I'd still wake up at three in the morning and lie in bed thinking about money problems (tuitions and income tax mostly) for an hour or two. Once or twice I suggested to Joan that time was running out and that if we were ever going to leave Litchfield we'd have to do it soon. She'd humor me, agreeing with any suggestions I might make, and gradually I'd forget about moving and settle back into what is, in fact, a very comfortable routine. It was about two years from the beginning of my crisis to its end. Even now, on rare occasions, I get a bit down but that, I've concluded, is perfectly normal. For me, the mid-life crisis is over.

Someone reading this chapter might say, "That wasn't a mid-life crisis he went through; it was an acute depression."

It's difficult to argue with that diagnosis. After all, about 20 percent of women and 10 percent of men go through a major depressive episode during their lifetime. Often even these major depressions aren't diagnosed as such. Minor depressions, which last only a few days or weeks, during which the symptoms—insomnia, a feeling of worthlessness, helplessness, and pessimism—are only moderate in severity, are almost never diagnosed. Many doctors think that depression is the most prevalent as well as the most underdiagnosed disease there is.

Admittedly, the male mid-life crisis may include all the symptoms of a depression, but there is almost always a major distinguishing feature. The man in depression gives up. He gets so down on himself that he surrenders. He is convinced he is no good and that nothing can be done about it. The man in mid-life crisis, however, no matter how down on himself he may be, comes fighting back. He dyes his hair; buys a sports car; starts an affair; raises hell in bars; argues with the boss; makes passes at his friends' wives; quits his job. In short, he does all those things that may get him into serious trouble. The man in depression simply lies on his bed of pain and bemoans his fate.

Admittedly, before the man in crisis starts to fight back, his condition may be almost indistinguishable from a depression. So what? When it hits the victim, he doesn't care what it's called. All he wants is to get better. That was my goal.

Some Other Men in Crisis

When I was through my crisis and could look back on it with perspective, I realized that although it had seemed to me a unique experience, that wasn't the case at all. I started talking about it with a few close friends, most of whom, I found, were well aware that for two years I hadn't been the old Bill Nolen they had known for years, and when I had finished talking they'd tell me of the mid-life crisis they were in or had gone through. Here are just a few typical stories:

(1) Charlie is forty-eight years old. His wife is forty-five. They have three children aged twenty, eighteen, and fourteen. Charlie runs an insurance agency.

Six months before our talk Charlie had begun worrying about his health. His father had had a heart attack when he was fifty-three and Charlie was certain he had heart trouble too. "I go to bed at night and my heart starts pounding," he said. "I can't get to sleep, wondering if I'm having a heart attack. I went to the doctor and he says my heart is all right, that I'm nervous, but I'm not sure I believe him. I just know this pounding means trouble. I can't get to sleep worrying about it."

Charlie had never been much of a drinker—"A few beers

on the weekend, that's all," he told me—but now he began to take two or three drinks almost every night. "To help me sleep," Charlie said. Unfortunately, as he soon discovered, the alcohol would help him get to sleep but then, after two or three hours, he'd wake up and find it difficult to get back to sleep. "I gave up on alcohol," he said. "I didn't particularly like it and it wasn't helping me sleep. I decided I could live with my heart pounding and the insomnia, though I hoped, of course, that it would go away."

For the last three months Charlie has been thinking of getting out of the insurance business. "I'm tired of it, Bill," he told me. "I've been at it twenty-five years now and if I don't quit soon it will be too late for me to do anything else. My father died at fifty-seven and my heart could go any time. It may be too late now, but I've got to give it a try. I don't want to spend my entire life selling insurance. It seems like such a waste."

(2) Ted is fifty-three. He's an internist and has a very successful practice. When he was forty-nine he went into a slump. "I was earning a lot of money," he said, "but I was bored with what I was doing. You know how it is, Bill, everyone thinks doctors have the most interesting profession imaginable, but after twenty-five years even medical practice begins to get wearing. I found myself hating to go to the office. I didn't even want challenging diagnostic problems. I preferred routine insurance examinations, things I could do without thinking. It was bad.

"And my home life was deteriorating. Our third and last child was off to college and Marie and I were free to come and go as we pleased. But now I found myself bored with life and not anxious to do anything. My interest in sex was close to zero and when I forced myself to be sexually active, about half the time I was impotent. I'd never had that problem before. Marie blamed herself for my sexual problem and that made me feel even worse. It wasn't her fault, I knew that, but it was difficult to convince her that she was blameless.

"I didn't know what to do to snap out of this slump. I was reluctant to go to a psychiatrist—embarrassed to admit I needed help—but when I found myself thinking about suicide, even casually, I knew I had to do something. Finally I swallowed my pride and called a psychiatrist to whom I'd previously referred several patients. I had never met him, which I figured was best. His reputation was excellent and he'd done a good job with the patients I'd sent him. It took time, but eventually I got straightened out.

"I wonder now if I'd have gotten better without his help. He agrees that I might have and I'll probably never be sure. I'm just glad that I'm back to what passes for normal. I've cut back a bit on my practice, not because of lack of interest but because I've developed, at his suggestion, another interest—painting. I'd enjoyed painting when I was in college but dropped it when I went to medical school. Now I'm back at it and enjoying every minute."

(3) Paul is the managing editor of a high-quality, closed-circulation trade journal aimed at people in the computer business. He has degrees in both chemical engineering and journalism and worked as an engineer for ten years before going to work at the magazine. He started as a senior editor in 1970 and has been managing editor since 1975. He is forty-seven years old and he and his wife, Mary, have three children, aged twenty, eighteen, and sixteen.

"About a year and a half ago," Paul told me, "I started getting restless. The magazine was doing very well—our circulation has grown steadily over the last ten years—but I wasn't getting as much satisfaction out of its success as I thought I should. I became a real grouch, tough for our editors and writers to work with. I didn't immediately realize what a pain I was becoming, but it wasn't long before it became obvious. One of our best editors quit and before he left he came into my office and told me in no uncertain terms that I was the cause of his dissatisfaction. 'You've become an unpredictable S.O.B.,' he told me; 'one day you're cheerful, the next you're so cranky that nothing pleases you. I'm getting out of here before I hit you.' He was furious.

"That night I told Mary what had happened, expecting her to tell me I was all right and that the editor was wrong. When she didn't comment I knew I was in trouble. I asked her if she thought I was unpredictable and cranky and she cried and said yes. We had a long talk that evening and the next day I went to our family doctor. He listened to my story, examined me, and asked me a lot of questions about my eating and sleeping habits, my sex life, and my interests other than my work and family. It wasn't till I had to answer these questions that I fully realized how much I had changed. I now had insomnia, my sex life had gone from active to almost inert, and I wasn't getting the exercise that I used to get. A year earlier, I had dropped my membership in the tennis club where I had been playing three times a week because, I said, I didn't have time. Now I knew that was just nonsense. I had lost interest in tennis, my work, and my family.

"When I realized what had happened to me I was determined to change. My doctor put me on what he called mood-elevating pills because he had decided I was in a depression. I guess I was, because after three weeks on the medicine I was feeling a lot better. In the meantime, at his suggestion, I was pushing myself to do things even when I didn't feel like doing them. I went back to tennis three times a week, worked hard at being nice to both my family and the people I work with, and tried my hand at writing for our magazine as well as managing and editing it. I thought for a while that maybe I was feeling better because I was doing all these things and so I asked him to take me off the medicine. When he did I began to slump again, so I went back on it. Six months later I went off the medicine again and didn't get depressed—if that's what my problem was—and I've been off all medication for the last six months.

"Those six months before I went to the doctor were six of the worst months of my life. And of Mary's life, she tells me. I didn't realize how I'd changed till that editor blew up at me; that was the greatest favor that anyone could have done for me. Thank heavens that's all behind me, at least for now. My doctor told me I might possibly have a recurrence later but I hope next time I'll realize what's happening and will make adjustments or get medical help quicker than I did this time. It's as if I lost six months of my life, and I don't have that much time to spare."

(4) Jerry owns a very successful plant that manufactures high-technology instruments. He is fifty-two now. He was forty-four when he went into crisis. "It started with sex, Bill," he told me. "I've always prided myself on being a sort of a stud. Alice and I had a very active sex life. At forty-four, after twenty years of married life and three kids, I suddenly became impotent. Not completely impotent, you understand, but once in a while I just couldn't get it up.

"That hit me hard. Alice didn't say anything and neither did I; I think now that might have been a mistake. We should have talked about it.

"Anyway we had this young woman, Sheila, working at the office. She was twenty-five, and a real good looker. She always gave me the big eye, so one night, when we had both worked late, I asked her if she'd like to have a drink with me. She said yes.

"Bill, you can't believe these younger women. It's a whole new ball game. We had a couple of drinks that first night; then I suggested dinner; Alice was playing bridge so I knew she wouldn't be home until midnight. Sheila said fine and, after dinner, when I drove her home, she invited me in for a nightcap. Some nightcap! I spent the night with her and I was as good as I had been ten years earlier. I could hardly believe how uninhibited these gals are.

"That one night opened a whole new world to me. I turned into a swinging young single; I admit it. Bought a toupee, got a flashy car, started hitting the singles spots. Alice knew, I suppose, but she didn't say anything. Not at first, anyway.

"Over the next year I had a hell of a time. I was like a new person. I guess I drank more than I should have, because one of our auditors showed me that our business was beginning to slip, and I recognized that my judgment wasn't as sharp as it had been, but I was having such a ball I hardly cared.

"Well, you know the rest of it. After two years, Alice blew the whistle. Said I'd been neglecting her and the kids—they were seventeen, fifteen, and fourteen then—and that I'd either have to straighten out or get out. She wasn't going to put up with things as they were.

"I could see she had a point, but I didn't want to go back. Gosh, you only live once. I wanted it all. I left. Alice's lawyers took me for plenty, but I thought it was worth it, at the time.

"Now, to tell you the truth, I'm not so sure anymore. I'm fifty-two now, and the singles joints aren't as much fun as they used to be. My oldest boy is out of college, and he hardly speaks to me. I guess he resents my not having gone to his high school football games. I can't say the younger two are close to me either. Probably my fault.

"Sheila and I have had a thing going for the last six months, but I'm not sure how it's going to work out. She's thirty-three and I'm fifty-two and I'm not as interested in the night club scene as she is. Another thing, she'd like to have a couple of kids and I'm not sure I want to go down that road again.

"To tell you the truth, Bill, I sometimes wonder if I didn't make a mistake six years ago. But at the time it sure seemed like the right thing to do."

(5) Leo is forty-five. He owns a combination restaurant and off-sale liquor store. He has never been married. "Marriage just never seemed like something I needed," he told me. "The store and restaurant have kept me busy most evenings, and I've had plenty of women friends. Marriage and kids and all that hassle just seemed like something I could do without. Most of the guys who come into my place for a beer or a drink after work are married and I never noticed them running home to their wives and kids.

"Now, though, I'm not so sure. For the last year I've been in a kind of slump. The business is going well but sometimes I ask myself, 'What's the point of it all?' I finish up at the restaurant, go home, catch a late movie on television and go to sleep about three in the morning. Sundays I usually have dinner with my mother; my dad died last year. I have a few buddies I can call on when I want to take in a Twins game or go see the North Stars, but I really don't know anyone except my mother who'd miss me much if I dropped dead of a heart attack tomorrow. No wife, no kids; sometimes it seems to me I'm working all my life for nothing. I keep telling myself it's not too late, that I can still find the right girl, get married, raise a family, but it isn't as easy as it sounds. I want the wife and the family, but I want my independence too. I'm not sure I could adjust to the demands of a family.

"What I do know is that I'm not sleeping as well as I used to and I'm drinking more than I should. I always had a rule for myself: no drinking on the job. Twice in the last month I broke that rule. Once I got moderately smashed watching the Vikings in the bar on a Sunday afternoon. The other time I got really blitzed when a couple of old buddies came in and we started reminiscing about our high school days.

"I don't know what's the matter with me. Here I am, forty-five years old, with a good business and plenty of money; I should have the world by the tail. Instead I'm in the pits. All I can think of is all I've got to look forward to is twenty more years of the same thing I've been doing for the last twenty. What's the point of it all?"

I knew what Leo's problem was: the same one I had had and the same one that all these other men had. He was in a mid-life crisis and he didn't even know it. Like all the rest of us, Leo needed help.

THREE

Making the Diagnosis:
The Physical Examination

One of the things people sometimes don't realize is that there are a lot of problems to which the medical profession doesn't have solutions. Not only specific scientific problems—a cure for cancer, for example, or even a cure for the common cold—but less tangible ones. Why, for example, are some people chronically overweight? What causes depression? Why does one person have a high pain threshold while another can hardly tolerate a hangnail? Not only do we lack answers to these questions, but we aren't even looking for them. These kinds of problems aren't particularly glamorous—no one dies of a low pain threshold—and they're difficult to bring into focus. It seems as if the answers probably depend on a combination of biochemical, physical, and psychological factors, and when causes are so complex they are difficult to unravel. It's easiest just to ignore them.

The mid-life crisis falls into this category. The signs and symptoms don't involve just one or even two systems of the body. When you're afflicted, the manifestations may be apparent in the circulatory system, the digestive system, the nervous system, the musculo-skeletal system, the reproductive system—virtually any or even every part of the body. Here, for example, is the way one forty-seven-year-old man described his condition. "I go to bed at night and as soon as I lie down my heart starts racing. I can even feel it skip beats. This frightens me, as you'd expect, and I have a terrible time getting to sleep. Most nights I take a Nembutal or a couple of drinks. Sometimes I need both.

"One thing that always used to put me to sleep was sex. My wife used to joke about it. 'Wham, bam, thank you ma'am,' she'd say. Lately though, I've had a hell of a time getting it up. Twice I couldn't do it and now I'm afraid to try.

"I'm even losing weight. My appetite is poor and I have bouts of diarrhea. I worry that I may have intestinal cancer; that's what killed my father."

The circulatory system, the reproductive system, the digestive system—all three have gone askew for this man. Nevertheless, I examined him and found nothing physically wrong. His blood pressure is 130/80, his heartbeat (as he sits quietly in my office) is regular, his blood hormone levels are just where they should be, and the barium enema shows a perfectly normal colon. Physically, he's fine. Physiologically, though, he's a mess. His body just isn't working properly.

Why? The fact is, we don't know. The easiest answer we can give—the one most doctors offer—is to say, "It's all in his head." After all, irregular heartbeats and/or a racing heart can be caused by nerves. So can diarrhea. So can loss of appetite. So can impotence. But when we say his problems are due to "nerves" we are really begging the question. The logical follow-up question is, "Why is this patient having a problem with his nerves?" and to that we have to answer, "I don't know." Perhaps it's a reaction to the circumstances of his life. He finds himself in what he perceives as a trap, he can't see any way out, and that causes anxiety, which in turn affects the nerves that go to all the other parts of his body. Maybe that's the answer. Maybe.

But another possibility is that something has happened to this man's body chemistry, particularly his brain chemistry. We are profoundly ignorant of how the brain works. We can throw around terms like neurotransmission and electro-transmission, caudate nucleus, basal ganglia, and substantia nigra, but if someone asks, "Tell me how, when I start to eat a pizza, the messages get to my chewing muscles, my salivary glands, my stomach, duodenum, small intestine, gall bladder, and pancreas, so that they're ready to take care of this conglomeration of pasta, anchovies, cheese, sausage, and tomatoes," no one in the world can answer that question. All we know is that it happens. Somehow, when you put that bite of pizza in your mouth, messages go out to all the proper areas. The stomach secretes just enough hydrochloric acid, the gall bladder squirts out the proper amount of bile, the pancreas pours out the proper amount of the appropriate enzymes, the small intestine starts churning at just the right speed to properly digest the pizza. It all works and is governed at a subconscious level.

Just in the last ten years we've discovered that the brain produces a group of complex, hormone-like substances called endorphins. We know that one of these endorphins acts in the body just as morphine does. Heaven alone knows what all the other endorphins do. Might there be an endorphin, or an imbalance of endorphins, that causes depression? Certainly. Might endorphins cause schizophrenia? That seems very possible. Could there be an endorphin or an endorphin imbalance that causes the male mid-life crisis? There certainly could be.

If it is an endorphin problem that produces the male mid-life crisis, could that problem in turn be caused by a viral infection? Yes. Could it simply be the result of the normal changes in brain cells that occur with aging? Definitely. Is it possible that the male mid-life crisis is a disease in the same sense that measles, pneumonia, chicken pox, and the common cold are diseases? Yes. Is it correct to say that we really don't know what it is that causes the male mid-life crisis? That is most emphatically correct.

Which does not mean, of course, that we can't treat the condition. We treat a lot of conditions for which we don't know the cause: cancer, sickle-cell anemia, schizophrenia, the common cold, are examples. It's always preferable to treat diseases by getting at their causes, but it's possible to do a reasonably good job even when we treat them indirectly. For example, until about forty years ago we didn't have any way to treat tuberculosis directly. Still, a lot of people recovered from tuberculosis. Sometimes we removed part of a lung, or used methods to temporarily collapse a lung and put it at rest, and the patient would get well. Often we'd send afflicted patients to sanitariums where, with rest, clean air, and good nutrition, they'd heal themselves.

Of course, once we acquired drugs that would kill the germ that caused tuberculosis, we were able to avoid surgery except in the very rare case, and the sanitariums where tuberculosis was once treated have all either been closed or turned into homes for the elderly. The number of people in the United States who will die from tuberculosis this year is infinitesimal in comparison to the number who annually died of tuberculosis fifty years ago.

Unlike tuberculosis, however, which we now know is caused by the mycobacterium tuberculosis and can be easily treated with streptomycin and other drugs, we haven't identified any one specific root cause for the male mid-life crisis (if, in fact, one exists), so treatment of the condition is just what it would be for any disease of undetermined cause: get the patient into the best possible general health, so that his own body (and mind) can fight off the condition. Simultaneously, treat the symptoms of the disease. If we do these things well, the patient should recover. Let's now consider in more detail both the diagnosis and treatment of the man in mid-life crisis.

II

The first thing a man in crisis should do is to get himself a thorough physical examination. Why? Because although he and his wife and his friends may be virtually certain that the man is going through a mid-life crisis and that he doesn't require any specific medical treatment, they may all be wrong. The mid-life crisis produces such a multitude of diverse symptoms that only a thorough examination by a competent physician can determine with certainty that the problem is, indeed, mid-life crisis. Besides, there is no law that says the man in mid-life crisis cannot also have some other illness. To treat a man for a mid-life crisis (which he may have) while ignoring the diabetes (which he may have simultaneously developed) could be disastrous.

Think how sad it would be if the man in crisis, after two years of misery, discovered that his problem was a physical one, easily treated. For example, one of the men to whom I spoke, whose crisis had been precipitated by increasing impotence, discovered, when he finally went for a thorough physical examination, that his impotence was due to a condition called Leriche's syndrome, in which the lower end of the aorta becomes plugged with arteriosclerotic plaques and the blood flow to the penis is so impaired that it is not possible to achieve erection. He had been going through a classic mid-life crisis (except, of course, that he hadn't become sexually involved with another woman), and he and his wife had been to three marriage counselors. Once the diagnosis was made, a vascular surgeon operated on his aorta and he was promptly cured of his crisis with all its related phenomena.

In the mid-forties, like it or not, our bodies begin to wear down. A thorough physical examination may reveal an unsuspected anemia, diabetes, hypertension, even a benign brain tumor, the only symptom of which has been depression. It's tough enough for a man in perfect health to get through a crisis; to try to fight it when he's not physically well can be devastating.

When you go for a physical examination, be certain that you get a good one. Go to an internist or a family practitioner who will do a thorough job. This does not necessarily mean that he will order a lot of blood tests and X-rays. It does mean that he will spend at least fifteen minutes talking with you, taking a complete medical history. Another ten or fifteen minutes should be devoted to the physical examination. If the doctor to whom you go for a complete examination doesn't spend at least half an hour with you, the chances are he hasn't done a thorough job.

There is one exception to this rule. If the doctor to whom you go is your family doctor, then he probably knows so much about you, having treated you previously, that he won't need to spend as much time as the doctor who is seeing you for the first time. However, it may be wise for the man in crisis to go to a doctor he does not know personally. He may find that he can speak more frankly to a stranger than to someone he knows well, particularly about any sexual problems he may be having. It is also possible that the doctor, seeing the patient for the first time, without any preconceived notions about the patient's health, will notice symptoms or signs that might be so familiar to the family doctor that he doesn't really see them.

If you asked me, or almost any doctor, to choose between taking a medical history or doing a physical examination in order to determine what, if any, problems the patient has, I'd choose the medical history. If you listen carefully to a patient's medical history, asking appropriate questions, you can usually narrow down the list of possible diagnoses to two or three, and perhaps just to the one diagnosis. That's why, for the male in crisis, it's so important to go to a doctor who is willing to really listen.

It is equally important that the patient be absolutely honest with the doctor. It always amazes me to find how often patients are less than truthful with their doctor. The doctor asks, "How much do you drink?" and the patient, who in reality drinks four or five highballs every night, answers, "Oh, I occasionally have one drink before dinner." The doctor asks, "How much do you smoke?" and the patient, a three-pack-a-day person, answers, "About half a pack a day." This tendency to try to deceive the doctor, particularly when it comes to drinking and smoking, is so prevalent that some doctors (I'm one of them) tend to suspect that every patient drinks or smokes, or does other things, twice as often as he says he does.

A patient who isn't honest with the doctor cannot expect to get optimum treatment. Any doctor will tell you that, despite the advent of CAT scanners, sophisticated blood tests, and computers, the patient's history remains the most valuable of all diagnostic tools.

If the man is over forty and has had any symptoms that suggest heart disease—or even if he thinks that his symptoms suggest heart disease—he should probably have not just an electrocardiogram but a stress electrocardiogram. An electrocardiogram tells the doctor how the heart will function at rest; but a stress electrocardiogram, taken while the patient is exercising on a treadmill, tells the doctor how well the patient's heart works under physical stress. That is what we're really interested in knowing. In the 1980s, with heart disease still by far the number one killer of middle-aged men, and with so many new drugs and/or surgical procedures that can be used to treat coronary artery disease (the most common form of heart disease), I think a stress electrocardiogram ought to be part of a complete physical examination of any man in mid-life crisis.

Other conditions that can produce symptoms similar to those of the man in crisis, or which will make those symptoms worse if they already exist, are anemia, hypothyroidism, diabetes, and depression. The blood test for anemia is simple and cheap and can be done immediately in the doctor's office. The test for hypothyroidism is a bit more expensive and has to be done in a laboratory more elaborate than most doctors have in their offices. Usually diabetes can be detected simply by doing a urine test for sugar, but in diabetes that first begins in middle age the urine test may not show sugar, even though the blood level of sugar is elevated. For the male in crisis a blood sugar test should be done. Oddly, some of the complications of diabetes—such as neuritis—may develop as rapidly in the patient with mild diabetes as in the patient with severe diabetes. Since diabetic neuritis is a common cause of impotence, it's well worth the few extra dollars the blood sugar test costs to make certain the male in crisis does not have diabetes.

I mention these three conditions—anemia, hypothyroidism, and diabetes—because they often develop insidiously, are frequently overlooked (hypothyroidism is much less common than the others), and produce an "all tired out" feeling that is so often already a problem for the man in crisis.

These three are easily detected, if the doctor remembers to look for them, but the fourth condition I mentioned earlier—depression—is probably the most insidious of all diseases and one for which there is not as yet a specific test. Many doctors consider depression the most common of all diseases and the one that most often is overlooked by physicians, particularly when it is only of moderate severity. When a man takes an overdose of sleeping pills or slashes his wrists, then the doctor will certainly consider the possibility that he's depressed. But when his only complaint is chronic tiredness, lack of interest in sex, and difficulty concentrating, the doctor may (probably will) just say, "Don't worry about it. We all get down now and again," when he really ought to make certain the man isn't suffering from depression.

Without getting too technical, let me first say that there are two kinds of depression: reactive depression and organic or endogenous (self-generated) depression. A reactive depression, as the name implies, is simply a normal reaction to an event that is upsetting. The death of a close friend, financial problems, job dissatisfaction can all cause depression. The depression is temporary and goes away with time or when the underlying problem is resolved.

An endogenous depression is one that comes on for no apparent reason. Current thinking is that the depression may be triggered by some as yet unidentified change in brain chemistry. The afflicted patient tends to feel worthless, helpless, and pessimistic. He may have any or all of the symptoms commonly associated with the male mid-life crisis. In fact, there are doctors who say that the male mid-life crisis is a form of depression, a claim with which I won't argue since it doesn't change anything as far as treatment is concerned. We don't know the exact cause of either the mid-life crisis or depression, so both are treated symptomatically.

It is important for the doctor who examines the male in crisis to decide whether the man does indeed have an endogenous depression. If so, either then or later it may be appropriate to prescribe mood-elevating, antidepressant medication, to go with the other supportive therapy that he needs.

Despite all the technical advances we've made in the world of medicine, it still remains an art as well as a science. The man in crisis and his wife need to be certain that the doctors to whom they go for a checkup haven't forgotten the art of medicine.

Let's suppose that the man in crisis does get a clean bill of health. His blood pressure is normal, his electrocardiogram (or even his stress test) shows that his heart is perfectly fine, his blood count is where it should be, and he's only five pounds overweight. Has he wasted the $50 or $100 he spent on the examination?

He has not. There's nothing like assurance that your health is optimal to erase that nagging little doubt tucked away deep in your mind that maybe there's a cancer buried away in your body, or a plugged artery just waiting to set off a heart attack. Men in crisis often have these worries, even when they don't verbalize them. The perfect gift for the man in crisis is a complete physical examination.

One suggestion I'd offer the wife of the man in crisis if her husband agrees to take the physical examination: call his doctor ahead of time and tell him about any signs or symptoms you've noticed. If his sexual activity is on the decline; if he's drinking too much; if he's just sitting around watching television on the afternoons when he used to be out playing golf, tell the doctor. You can bet the man won't tell the doctor these things. He may not even be aware of them, and if he is he won't think of them as medical problems. One thing I can almost guarantee: if neither wife nor husband mentions these problems to the doctor, the doctor won't ask about them. Oh, he might ask, "How much do you smoke? How much do you drink?" but he won't pursue these subjects. It's the extremely unusual doctor who regularly questions his male patients about sex life or drinking habits or any of the other crisis problems, unless he has been advised to do so.

It's a very good idea for the wife of the man in crisis to also have a physical examination. One psychologist to whom

I spoke was most emphatic about this. "Often the wife of a man in crisis is, herself, getting near the menopausal age. Only about 15 percent of menopausal women get hot flashes, but other changes occur at menopause time that aren't as obvious. As the hormone balance shifts, subtle changes in body chemistry may be occurring—things we recognize only by their symptoms—which may include depression, increase or decrease in sex drive and, of course, changes in the vaginal and perineal tissues. A woman in the throes of a menopausal syndrome trying to help a man in mid-life crisis may truly be a case of the blind leading the blind. Pulling her out of her problem may be as simple a matter as writing a prescription for a low dose of estrogen. If she's anemic—and a lot of women as they approach menopause have heavy menstrual periods, which may make them significantly anemic— then she's going to be chronically tired. You can imagine how difficult it would be for a woman in that condition to deal with a man in crisis.

"Frankly, I feel so strongly about the importance of a thorough physical examination for the wife of the man in crisis, that ordinarily I'll refuse to counsel a woman who won't have a physical. It would be a waste of time for both of us if we were to spend hours working on psychological problems when hormones and/or an iron tablet could almost remedy the situation."

I am not one of those doctors who advocate regular physical examinations for men or women. My general policy is to say, "Don't go looking under rocks. If you feel well, you probably *are* well. Stay away from the doctor unless you're having symptoms."

The man in crisis, however, does have symptoms. He may not think they are physical in origin, but without a complete physical examination he can't be sure. His symptoms may come solely from the psychological effects of the mid-life crisis; they may be in part due to the crisis and in part to some physical disorder; they may even be due only to a physical disorder. He needs the physical examination to be certain he's getting appropriate treatment. And his wife, who is assuredly going to be under a lot of stress while her husband is going through his crisis, needs a complete physical examination to be certain that she is in optimum condition to cope with a taxing situation.

Physical examinations for both the man in crisis and his wife may be the best investment they can possibly make.

FOUR

The Man in Crisis and His Family: Problems and Support

WIFE

Once the man in crisis has had a physical examination, and his illnesses, if any, have been or are being properly treated, it's time to consider what should be done next to help him through his crisis. The first thing the man in crisis needs (actually he needs this along with or even before his physical examination) is someone with whom he can talk about his problems—a sympathetic listener. If there is one word that describes what a man in crisis most needs, communication is that word. The person on whom the married man depends most for communication, to whom he is most likely to turn when he needs a sympathetic listener, is his wife.

It frightens me to think of some of the breakdowns in interpersonal communication that occur between men and their wives. For example, when I was doing research for this book, one subject I investigated in detail was impotence. Among those I interviewed were two psychologists who spent a lot of time trying to decide whether men were suitable candidates for penile prostheses. "Most of these men have been impotent for at least one year," one of the doctors said. "I'll bet that in 95 percent of cases neither husband nor wife has ever mentioned the subject. They certainly haven't discussed it. All of a sudden the sex life stops, and no one says anything. Don't you find that difficult to believe?"

I might have, if I hadn't known that when our sex life declined from active to nothing, neither Joan nor I mentioned it for six months, and then only casually. I guess, like other couples, we thought that if we ignored the problem it would go away.

Now I realize that in most marriages communication seems to gradually fade away after the first few years. Husbands and wives still talk, of course, but usually about practical matters—can we afford a new car; what should we have for dinner; should we vacation in the winter or the summer—or about children, if there are any. And as the children get older, they tend to become the topic of conversation 90 percent of the time: Is it too soon for Mary to date? Why isn't Paul going out for track? Who told Jimmy he could take the car? Husband-and-wife communication after five years rarely deals with their personal feelings about themselves and each other.

Ask yourself this: when did you last sit down with your spouse and tell him or her exactly how you were feeling? It has been years, I'll bet. You've learned to read each other's minds, or behave as if you can.

Am I exaggerating? I think not. Before my mid-life crisis I know that I had never said to Joan: "How are you feeling? Are you satisfied with the way our lives are going? Do you think there are any changes we ought to make? Are any of the things I'm doing distressing or irritating to you?" I hadn't asked questions like those in the twenty-five years we were married. I'd have felt silly if I had.

Nor had Joan asked me such questions. She'd have felt as

silly as I, I'm sure. Husbands and wives can take each other
for granted. They don't need to ask probing questions. That's
the way we live our lives.

And that's one of the reasons we have mid-life crises. If
Joan and I had made it a regular practice to sit down together
for an hour twice a week to really talk, maybe I'd have avoided
some of the problems my crisis brought to both of us. Perhaps
if I had said, "Joan, I don't know if I can take this call schedule any longer; I think it's wearing me out," we'd have made
some changes that would have helped me avert crisis time.
Maybe not completely, but in part. I'll never know.

It's odd that once two people get married, they immediately run out of things to say to one another. Before they're
married they take long walks together; plan the future; spend
hours on the telephone; rarely tire of each other's company;
and spend much of their time together talking.

Once they're married, communication declines rapidly.
After ten years of marriage, monosyllables constitute the bulk
of most husband-wife conversations. This isn't universally
true, of course, but it applies to a great many marriages.

What happens is that husband and wife think they know
each other so well that conversation isn't necessary. He knows
she likes to play bridge on Thursday evenings; she knows he
enjoys playing poker at the golf club on men's night. She
knows he likes to watch pro football on Sunday afternoon;
he knows she likes to watch the women's golf tour. They both
enjoy "60 Minutes" and they both like movies, though not
always the same ones. So what's there to talk about?

Plenty. Chances are your wife would like to know how
things are going in your business world; you'd probably like
to know if home life is beginning to bore her or if she's having
problems with her job. She'd like to know what movie you'd
like to see on Saturday night; you might like to know whether
the book she is reading is interesting. There ought to be
hundreds of interesting things for a husband and wife to talk

about, but after a few years of marriage they get out of the habit of talking much.

When the mid-life crisis hits, this lack of communication often makes what might have been a minor problem into a major one. Just think what might happen if, early on, the man—we'll call him Jim—said to wife, Irene, "Let's talk for a while. Lately I've been feeling lousy." If she says, "Fine, maybe we can do it tomorrow evening; I've got my bridge club tonight," that's an opportunity missed that will probably never be regained. If, instead, she says, "Fine, Jim, let me just phone and get someone to substitute for me at bridge club," and, after the call, draws a chair up next to his, they may get right to the source of the trouble. Maybe he'll tell her that he is tired of his job. Perhaps she'll ask him why his sexual interest seems to have declined. Maybe they'll agree that their nightly cocktail hour, which has recently begun to run to two hours, ought to be replaced by a long walk.

When Jim tells Irene that his job has become routine and boring, she can give him support and sympathy. If he's wondering if he should make a career change, she can suggest possibilities and join him as he considers the pros and cons of any move. Together they can accomplish much more than either can alone.

Most counselors believe, and I certainly agree, that communication can be the key to preventing mid-life crises from ending in disaster. The man and woman who will sit down together at least three times a week for half an hour and unburden their souls to each other will avoid many of the problems that other couples encounter, particularly in mid-life.

Chances are that you will protest that you talk that much now. I doubt it very much. One on one? Half an hour at a time? Three times a week? No other distractions? Completely open and honest with each other? If that were true I doubt very much that you'd be reading this book.

What do you talk about? Let's be specific. If either of you is bothered by something in the other's behavior, for heaven's sake say it. John O'Hara once wrote in a short story something to the effect that most marriages break up over little things. As examples, he mentioned the way one husband always let a little bit of his soft-boiled egg drip from his spoon as he ate in the morning. That little idiosyncrasy almost drove his wife crazy. For one man it was his wife's habit of leaving just a wisp of toilet paper floating in the bowl after she'd used the bathroom. Done a hundred or a thousand times, little things like this can drive someone up the wall. What's sad is that the offenders don't even know they are offending. The injured party has to speak up or nothing gets changed. It's these little things that make us testy so that we explode more vehemently than we should when a big problem arises.

I told Joan at least fifteen years ago that when I buy a Coca-Cola between sets of tennis or rounds of golf I hate it when she says, "I don't want a whole Coke; just give me a sip." I want the entire Coke. I'm quite willing to buy her her own Coke and, if she can't finish it, either I will or it will be thrown away. But I'm not sharing my Coke with anyone. She doesn't ask anymore for a sip of mine or, if she does, we both laugh; she knows she isn't going to get it.

Nor am I going to get the Variety section of the Sunday newspaper while she's reading the front section. She used to give it to me, but I finally realized that it bothered her. "Would you rather I wait for the paper until you've read the whole thing?" I asked, and she agreed that she would. No problem. I just wish she had told me five years earlier that reading the paper in pieces bothered her. It would have saved her five years of unnecessary irritation. I'm willing to wait until she's finished.

There are two rules that I dearly love: Rule #1 is, "Don't sweat the little things." Rule #2 is, "They're all little things."

What I find very amusing about these rules, which practically everyone has heard of, is that we say, "They are so right," but we hardly ever follow them. We do sweat the little things—it's human nature to do it—so why not change the little things when we can?

What else should you talk about? The big things: your job; her job; the children; your hopes, and your fears. I think I'll always remember one woman of fifty who told me that she had always wanted to visit San Francisco, she'd read so much about the scenery and the great restaurants, but she guessed they'd never get around to it since her husband's business trips always took him to the East Coast. When I casually mentioned to the husband his wife's desire to visit San Francisco he said, "That's no problem. I've got a slow week next week and it's supposed to be nice there in October. We'll go." His wife literally broke into tears of joy when he told her.

Touching, but really sad. All she would have had to do ten years earlier was to say, "Charlie, I'd really like to go to San Francisco sometime if we can arrange it," and she'd have been there. But Charlie wasn't a mind reader and he was perfectly content with his semiannual visits to New York, Boston, and Miami. How could he guess where his wife really wanted to go?

That is one of our problems. After we've been married a while we begin to act as if we are mind readers, particularly where our spouse is concerned. One starts a sentence, the other finishes it. We communicate in monosyllables. The trouble is, we often get the message wrong.

Stop trying to read each other's minds. Stop finishing each other's sentences. Sit and listen, listen, listen to each other. It's amazing how much you'll discover about this person you thought you knew so well. It's equally amazing to discover how much relief from emotional distress the man in crisis can find simply by talking—*really* talking—to his wife.

CHILDREN

Should children be included in some of the discussions of crisis problems? If the children are young—twelve or under—as a general rule I don't think it's a good idea. Young children don't want to think that their parents have problems. They want to believe that Mommy and Daddy are both omniscient and omnipotent. Why disillusion them? They have a lot of years to live when they'll be well aware that adults, including their parents, have plenty of problems.

If the children are teen-aged or older, then the answer depends on how obvious the problems are, whether or not they're affecting the child, and—most important—on the child himself. Some children are very sensitive to personality changes in their parents. Others live as if the parents existed only to feed and shelter them.

It also depends on how comfortable the parents feel in discussing their personal problems with their children. My children ranged in age from sixteen to twenty-four when I was in the depths of my crisis, but only Mary, our sixteen-year-old, was living at home all of the time. The rest were home only in the summer or on holidays. Mary was so caught up in her high school activities—she is one of those kids who get involved in every possible school activity—that we weren't sure she had even noticed I was in a slump. We decided to wait to talk with her until she asked Joan, "Is something wrong with Dad?" or in some other way showed concern about me. That situation never arose.

If the older kids had been home I suspect that we would have said something to them. In fact, on a couple of occasions I did talk with Jody, then twenty-three, about my restlessness, and she said, "Then why don't we just move some place else?" I explained why, telling her how difficult it would be to start a new career in a new city, or even to build a new surgical practice somewhere else, but she didn't seem to think these problems were insurmountable. I suppose they weren't, but they certainly seemed greater to me than they did to her.

The trouble with talking to children of any age about mid-life crisis problems is that their entire perspective on life is so different from that of their parents that they are likely to have difficulty understanding what's so major about the problem. Young men and women think they can accomplish anything. If they could see things as a fifty-year-old sees them, they'd probably go into a terrible slump. In fact, if they saw things as we see them, then they'd be having what amounted to a teen-age mid-life crisis. Why inflict our problems on them?

My insomnia, excessive drinking, and general apathy were not problems that directly affected our children, so we never discussed those problems with them. Other parents might have felt differently and might have chosen to talk about their problems with their children. If that's how parents feel, then it would probably be the right thing to do.

This seems like an appropriate place to write briefly about the way Joan and I have raised our children. Let me first say that I don't think there are any universally applicable rules for raising children. All relationships depend on the person-alities of the individuals involved. It is self-defeating to force yourself to treat your child in some particular way just be-cause some book says that is how most parents treat a child of that age. Children can tell when adults are behaving in a natural way and when they're faking it. So now I'll make an exception to my rule that there are no rules: never try to fool your children. You'll lose their trust; besides, you can't do it.

With six children born in such rapid sequence, Joan and I never had time to think about how we were going to manage this one as opposed to that one. We just did what came naturally. When a baby cried we tried to comfort him or her. When two cried simultaneously, if only one of us was around we concentrated on the one that seemed most miserable. If three or more were crying, some of them had to get over their problems by themselves.

As they grew older, and personality differences became increasingly apparent, we made whatever adjustments were necessary. For example, during grade and high school some of the kids were breakfast eaters and some weren't. We never had family breakfasts because I don't eat breakfast and Joan doesn't eat until she has had coffee and a couple of cigarettes. I've always figured that kids will eat when they're hungry and that whatever appeals to them (within limits) will probably give them all the nutrition they need. So we made available what food we thought was appropriate and gave it to them on a take-it-or-leave-it basis. If they didn't like what we had, they could prepare something for themselves. When there are six children and two adults eating dinner together most evenings, no one gets to order from a menu. As it turned out, Julius ate just toast and raspberry jam for breakfast for about three years and had hot dogs just about every night for dinner. Now, as a young man, he seems as healthy as the other five.

We've always had a lot of fun with our children, but not until they got into their twenties did we ever treat them as we did our adult friends. The basement has always been their place, and the ground floor is ours. They can play their music on the basement stereo; on ours we listen to jazz and musicals. We've skiied with them; Joan has shopped with the girls; I've played hockey with the boys; they've all read the magazines and many of the books that are always around the house. I think we're very close to them, and they feel the same way, but I know that they are also independent people. We've shared what it seemed natural to share. The problems of crisis time didn't fall into that category.

In my case—and that's the case I know best—my six children, all of whom I love very much, were big problems for me as I went through my crisis. When I was fifty the six children were almost completely financially dependent on me. The oldest was working, sporadically, but hadn't yet settled into anything that could be considered a steady job. The next oldest was one year out of college and bouncing from one poorly paying position to another. The other four were in school. I had to work as hard as I could just to earn the money to pay for board, room, and tuition for the four youngest and to help out the two oldest. This financial burden was a heavy and wearing one.

Should I have said, "To hell with it. Let them earn their own college educations, or do without?" Maybe, but I don't think so. I've known parents, a lot of them, who have done that. To those parents, obligations to their children ended when the children reached eighteen. I suspect that the parents of these parents had also cut them off at eighteen. But my parents had sent my two sisters and my brother through college and had sent me through college and medical school. They'd done that at no small sacrifice to themselves, something I hadn't realized until I was faced with the education problem. My father earned a decent living as a lawyer, but certainly not enough money so that he could educate us and at the same time live in the style that I know now he would have enjoyed. No luxurious vacations, no new Cadillacs, no fur coat for my mother. He'd have liked those things, but he never got them. He could have had them if he had said to us, "Educate yourselves."

I remember talking with my father in 1958, just a year before he died. I was a resident surgeon at Bellevue then, and he was still giving me $200 a month to help me support my family. I didn't realize then how much of a sacrifice he was making in sending me that money. One of my great regrets has been that I never appreciated it enough to adequately thank him for it. My brother, Jimmy, and my sister Judy were both in college at the time. My father, visiting us in New York, said, "Billy, if I ever get all you kids educated I'm going to cash in my life insurance, move to Ireland, and write." His life insurance was about all he had that could be converted into cash. He died in 1959, at fifty-eight. He didn't live long enough to make that move to Ireland.

What should the man in crisis do about his children? Obviously, if they're still in high school, he'll feel an obligation to support them; if he doesn't feel that obligation he might be taken to court by his wife to see that he accepts his responsibility, and the court will see to it that he does. But what if he's fifty or so and one of the problems that is weighing him down is the expense of educating the kids? Should he tell them, "I'm sorry, but you're going to have to find ways to educate yourselves."

Maybe he should. If worries about education money are so bad that they're giving him insomnia, driving him to an increased alcohol consumption, throwing him into a depression, then the price is too great a one to pay. Children are resourceful. They'll find a way to get an education, if they really want one. My brother said to me, just a year or so ago, "I'd a lot rather have gone to a state college and had Dad around for a few more years, than to have gone to Harvard and have him die so young." I can't say positively that the burden of educating all of us shortened my father's life, but it's possible that it was a factor.

On the other hand, even though I realized, and still do, that educating and helping out my children is a financial burden, which adds a considerable amount of stress to my life, I have the feeling that if I said, "I'm bowing out, you're all on your own," I'd feel so guilty that that in itself would be a terrible source of stress. Talk about being caught between a rock and a hard place! Kids will put the man in crisis there every time.

The only piece of advice I can offer, admittedly of limited helpfulness, is this: decide what you're going to do—help them out or toss them out—and once the decision is made, forget it. Don't dwell on all the "what ifs." It won't do any good.

Remember, one of the things the male in crisis is thinking about is his mortality. He knows that he is going to pass this way only once. He wants to get as much out of life as he can. He may think, "Why should I give up my happiness so that my kids can get an education so that they can grow up to pass up happiness so that their kids can get an education?" It's a darn good question. The answer to it will depend on how you define happiness.

One thing the man in crisis must be certain not to do is to shift on to his child or children the desires and aspirations that he once had and now realizes he won't achieve. This is a very common error. One man of fifty, who in his crisis became acutely aware that he was never going to become president of the company for which he worked, began pressuring his daughter into getting her M.B.A. when she wanted very much to get to work, with her B.A., in the publishing industry. He insisted that getting an M.B.A. would one day give her a chance to move higher in the publishing world than he had been able to go in his company. He may have been right, but it wasn't fair to his daughter to push her where she didn't want to go, just because of his disappointment.

Another friend, forty-seven, fed up with his life as an engineer, started pushing his son, then in college, to switch to pre-med rather than engineering. "That's the life," the man said. "Doctors really do things for people. That's what you ought to do." His son, wisely, stuck with engineering, which he found very appealing.

In the mid-life crisis it's easy to fall into this trap. The man looks at his career, tries to figure in retrospect where he went wrong (as he sees it), and then—unable at this stage of his life to overcome what he perceives as the errors that led him to his current disappointment—tries to live his life again, vicariously, through his children. It's not a realistic plan and it is certainly most unfair to his children.

Even sadder is the situation in which the man in mid-life crisis, who has for several years been counting on his children to accomplish the things he didn't, suddenly realizes that his children have no desire to follow the career he has chosen for them, or aren't capable of doing so. The daughter he hoped would be a doctor decides she doesn't even want to go to college. Her SATs aren't very good anyway and, at nineteen, she wants to marry her boy friend who is working as a mechanic at a local garage. The son, who was supposed to take over his father's construction business, turns out to have his mother's bookish temperament and wants to get a Ph.D. in philosophy. All the dreams the man had for his children disappear, just as he hits mid-life.

It can be a devastating blow. Some men literally force their children to at least begin the careers they planned for them. Almost invariably, this proves to be a disaster. A child, pushed into a career he or she doesn't want, won't do well at it. Then everyone is miserable.

Parents should not live life vicariously through their children. Those children are going to be adults with their own personalities and desires. Because of the genetic similarities, and the environment in which they were reared, they may follow in their parents' footsteps. They may even surpass their parents in accomplishment. If that happens, wonderful! But certainly no parent should count on it. We all have to live our own lives, and that includes our children. The man in crisis who has been, or becomes, dependent on his children to fulfill his dreams is making a very serious mistake.

PARENTS

The parents of the man in crisis, if they're alive, are likely to be elderly. If he's lucky, his parents will have enough retirement income to live in reasonable comfort; if he's very lucky, they may even be able to help him. But if they haven't the income to live comfortably, then what? It can be a tough decision. Does he take his parents to live with him and his family? Does he send them the money he and his wife would like to use for the treats he feels they now deserve? Or does he leave his parents to get by as best they can?

There are no right or wrong answers to those questions. You have to think about them, discuss them, and decide. My mother is a very active eighty-three-year-old who lives alone in a small apartment. One piece of advice she has given me, my brother, and my sisters many times over the years is, "Don't mix generations." She thinks the idea of the "extended family" that is becoming so fashionable these days—grandparents, parents, children, all under the same roof—is a lot of nonsense. "Your father's father lived with us for fourteen years," she says, "and he made a lot of my life miserable. He wanted things done his way, and I wanted to do them mine. The biggest mistake I ever made was in agreeing to let him live with us.

"Don't do it," she says. "Don't take me or any other parent into your home. Generations don't mix."

Not everyone will agree with this, I suspect. I'm sure there are many homes where three or even four generations live happily together, but I sometimes wonder if all these extended family households are as jolly and happy as they seem to be.

There is hardly a man who doesn't look at his father and mother and say to himself, "That's how I may be twenty-five or thirty years from now." As far as health is concerned, if his parents are still robust and active in their late sixties or seventies, this will be a cheering thought. However, if one or both of them are suffering from crippling arthritis or incapacitating emphysema or heart disease, he may worry that this will be his fate; after all, their genes are *his* genes. If he's wise, he'll do what he can to avoid these eventualities, exercise regularly, for example, or give up smoking.

And if his parents are having financial problems, it may depress him, but it should also stimulate him to do some serious financial planning to avoid, if he can, the predicament in which they find themselves.

There's no doubt that having parents who are in trouble may deepen the depression of the man in crisis, but it ought also to provoke him into doing things that he might not otherwise do to protect himself and his family. What is the saying? "Those who don't learn from history are doomed to repeat it."

Logically, one would think that a child would imitate the traits of each parent that seem admirable and try hard to avoid those that seem to have caused the parents trouble. I know, for example, a man whose father had regularly driven each car that he bought until the car actually collapsed of rust and general degeneration. This man now makes a regular practice of buying a new car every year; as a child, he hated to have to drive or be driven in his father's heap.

We can laugh at this example—my friend does—but it isn't unusual. We probably all know men whose fathers were heavy drinkers who are total or near total abstainers in adult life; they saw what troubles alcohol brought to their fathers and strive to avoid it. On the other hand, we probably all know men who drink heavily, following in the pattern of their parents. Why one man chooses to imitate a destructive parental habit while the other strives to avoid it is such a complex matter that I don't believe anyone has as yet unraveled it.

Sometimes the imitation seems to be sex-oriented. For

example, I don't smoke cigarettes and neither do our three sons. Joan, however, smokes three packs a day, and all our daughters smoke. I don't want to read too much into this one example, but it seems so obvious I can't help mentioning it.

Our parents are an example of what history, at least potentially, holds in store for us. All of us, particularly the man in crisis, should learn from the experiences of our parents.

The parent problem, if there is one, is likely to be complicated. It may involve anywhere from one to four parents and any number of brothers and sisters. Some of the children may be better off financially than the others; some may have better rapport with their parents than their siblings. It's impossible to formulate any general rule for the man in crisis to follow when it comes to his relationship with his or his wife's parents, or even their uncles and aunts. The only rule that applies is the same one that applies to children: once you've made the decision, once you've decided how much help you are willing and able to contribute, do it and then forget about it. To continuously dwell on a problem to which there is no certain, absolutely correct answer is a futile drain on one's energy. That is a luxury the man in crisis simply cannot afford.

FIVE

The Man in Crisis Outside His Family: Problems and Support

THE SINGLE MAN

What about the man who is single because he has never married or because he is divorced, widowed, separated, or gay? He may have a close friend—male or female, live-in or not—who acts as a surrogate for a wife and will provide most of the support he needs to get him through a crisis. If he doesn't have such a friend, he may be in serious trouble.

The single men—and they constitute an ever-increasing portion of the middle-aged segment of society—have most of the problems that married men have, and a few others as well. They not only worry about lack of advancement in their jobs, but in middle age the heterosexuals begin to wonder if they should have married, stayed married, remarried, and/or had children.

For the homosexual who does not have a permanent companion as he reaches middle age, but has only casual friends or lovers, the situation is much the same. As he becomes older and is in crisis, it is very difficult for *any* man to change

64

his life-style. If he does not have a mate, he badly needs someone else with whom he can talk over his problems.

Unattached men tend to be more concerned about changes in their physical appearance. Those with permanent mates don't have to find a companion; they already have one who isn't likely to leave them because they get a little careless about their grooming or put a few pounds on around the middle. A gentle suggestion from the mate to take better care of themselves may be all that is required.

However, the man who lives alone may be and probably is looking for a companion. One of the things that make people attractive to other people is appearance. All other things being equal, the man with the huge belly and the bulbous nose has to work harder to attract a companion than the man who is trim and handsome. This is just one of the many problems that may be more burdensome for the single man. From whom can he receive support?

From professional counselors or from support groups of one sort or another. As we shall see, these sources (support groups in particular) can be of enormous help to single men— heterosexual or gay—but they can also be very helpful for married men. As those who have been or are now married know, even with the most supportive wife there may be subjects that a man is reluctant to talk about. Sometimes, they are the things that trouble him most.

Perhaps, for example, he doesn't want to burden her with his financial problems. Maybe he can't bring himself to admit to her how disappointed he is that he was passed over for a promotion. He may be so embarrassed by his impotence that he simply cannot discuss it openly with her. There are times when it's easier for a man to talk to other men about his problems than it is to talk to a woman, even if the men are strangers and the woman is someone close to him. What are the alternatives, for all men—married or single—to talking things out with a mate?

PSYCHOTHERAPY

One option is to go to a psychotherapist. Psychologists, psychiatrists, family counselors, sex therapists, clinical social workers, and pastoral counselors are all available. The advantage of going to such people is not only that they are professional, and have almost certainly previously counseled people with similar problems, but also that the one chosen does not personally know the man in crisis. It's often easier to talk to a stranger about personal problems than it is to talk to someone whom you're going to see frequently or occasionally under other circumstances.

We often see cartoons showing someone sitting on a bar stool confiding in a bartender, looking for advice. That often happens. In fact, some mental health associations provide training for bartenders so they can identify people with serious emotional problems and refer them for further help. People talk to bartenders about their troubles because usually the bartender is someone they know only as a bartender. They can tell him their troubles because they aren't going to see him again, except in the bar. And, of course, they've usually had a drink or two and some of their usual inhibitions are gone.

Professional counseling, unfortunately, is usually expensive. Psychiatrists and psychologists generally charge at least $75 an hour. That's more than most of us can pay. Group therapy is usually less expensive, but if the man doesn't like one or more of the people in the group this may not be satisfactory. Professional counseling is certainly worth investigating, and the man in crisis may find it to be just the sort of help he needs.

One word of warning: in some states there is very little regulation of counselors. Virtually anyone can put up a sign advertising himself or herself as a counselor. Anyone seeking professional counseling should be sure to ask the counselor what his or her qualifications are.

If he can't afford or doesn't want professional counseling there are two other sources of support the man in crisis should consider.

SUPPORT GROUPS

A support group, as I've already mentioned, is one. In some cities there are meeting places where men in mid-life crisis can go to meet and talk with other men in the same situation. In Minneapolis the meeting place is called the Men's Center. I spent several hours talking with a man who had been very active in the Men's Center. I'll call him Pat Foley. He's thirty-five years old, a building contractor, married, with three children.

"The Men's Center has been in existence since 1977," Pat told me. "We used to rent a room in the downtown area, but when the city shut down one of the junior high schools, they made the building available for nonprofit organizations to use without charge. We have quite a large room—one of the old classrooms—for our use. In a way I'm sorry we made the move because the school is on the south side of the city, not quite as easily accessible as when we were right downtown. But the big advantage is that it's free. In 1981 we lost most of our funding, so we really can't afford any unnecessary expenditures."

I told Pat I was interested in hearing about what support they offered men in crisis. "That would fit under the general issues group," he said. "At least initially. What the man in crisis ought to do is come to one of our Thursday night meetings. It's very informal. There's no need to make a reservation or anything like that. Just show up at the Men's Center at 7:00 P.M., but don't be late; we start the meeting at 7:00 and then we lock the door so we won't be disturbed until the meeting ends. It runs until 9:00.

"Generally about twelve to fifteen men show up. We try not to have more than seven or eight men in a group, so we usually split into two groups. Some of the men will have been to previous meetings, a few will be there for the first time. We try to have one or two facilitators there for each group."

"What's a facilitator?" I asked.

"A facilitator is a fellow who has been in a support group for a while and has gone through a program to learn how to run a group. There aren't any special educational requirements. His big job is just to keep the meeting going. Any time you have six or seven men sitting around talking about their problems, it's easy for the group to get stuck on one subject or for one person to do most of the talking. The facilitator interrupts to get the conversation flowing again when that happens.

"Often the men who are there for the first time don't say much. In fact, they might not say anything. That's fine. We know that after one or two meetings they'll be more relaxed and join in the discussion. They'll usually get plenty out of just listening."

"What sort of subjects do they talk about?" I asked.

"Almost anything," Pat said, "their jobs, their wives, their children, anything that may be bothering them. Usually they'll talk about their feelings. The other night, for example, one man said, 'I've been feeling really insecure lately. I expected my company to send me to a convention and instead they sent one of my co-workers.' Then someone else said, 'Hey, that same thing happened to me, and to make it worse the person they sent was a woman, younger than I. I really had trouble dealing with that, until I realized that that didn't mean I was incompetent. I have no control over decisions made by others. I realized I was doing my job well. I also finally realized that I didn't really care about going to the convention; that, in fact, conventions bored me. I'd rather be home with my family.' Just knowing that the second man had had a similar experience made the first fellow feel better.

"Whenever you get a group of men together you almost invariably find that whatever problem one has, someone else in the group has also had. They've shared similar experiences and had similar emotional responses to them. It's always a relief to know that you aren't alone in this world. Sure, you realize that theoretically that's true; but now you know one real live human being who has actually been through what you're going through. That's consoling."

"What's the age range of the men who come to these meetings?" I asked.

"Anywhere from the late twenties to the late fifties," Pat said. "They're also from all sorts of backgrounds. We'll have carpenters, business executives, doctors, cab drivers—just about any work background you can think of—in various groups.

"What happens, usually, is that after two or three meetings half a dozen men will find that they get along particularly well with each other. Then they may decide to form a group of their own. We encourage that. They'll pick a time that is convenient for all of them and will arrange to meet at one of their homes, each taking a turn as host. The Men's Center will provide a facilitator for their first two meetings; after that, they're on their own."

"How long do these groups generally stay together?"

"That varies a lot, as you can imagine. We suggest that they make a commitment for three months. After that, they can take a look at what they're getting out of the meetings and either continue or drop out. Some groups have kept going for a couple of years. One person may drop out and someone else may join. Most of the men find the support they get from the group very helpful.

"We also have special interest support groups that meet at the center. We have a gay men's group, a parenting group, and a group for unemployed men. For a while we had two groups for unemployed men. Being unemployed is a devastating blow to a man's morale, especially after he's been a worker and the chief supporter of a family for years. Getting laid off really gives some men a terrible feeling of worthlessness. If there's ever a time when men need support it's after they've lost a job."

"Support groups sound fine to me," I said, "but I wonder how well they'd work in smaller cities and towns. After all, Minneapolis has half a million population and, even so, you have only twelve or fifteen men showing up at your open meetings. I wonder if you could find enough men to form a support group in a smaller place."

"Possibly not," Pat said, "though you have to realize that our Men's Center has practically no money. We used to get some funding from industry so that we could at least keep a secretary to answer the phone. Now we only have volunteers. And we don't advertise; most people don't even know the Men's Center exists. I think we would attract perhaps ten times as many men if we publicized our place. As it is, we have only one room so we couldn't really handle a huge group.

"You also have to remember that we have other support groups that focus on one issue. The gay support group is always well attended. As our society has become more open and more tolerant of homosexuality there are a lot of men who want to come out of the closet, but need help to do so. Talking to other men who have finally admitted they were gay, after years of suppressed and concealed homosexuality, can be of great help.

"You're particularly interested in the male mid-life crisis. I think you'd be surprised at how many men in mid-life have suppressed homosexuality to compound their other problems. Many of them have been living straight lives for years. Suddenly, at forty-five or fifty, possibly with a wife and children, they confront their homosexuality. What are they going to do about it?"

"What do they do?" I asked.

"Different things," Pat told me. "It depends on their circumstances. If he's married and has young children, the man may just continue to lead a straight life, taking a chance on a homosexual encounter every now and then. He may suppress his homosexuality entirely, if he's strong enough. At the other extreme, particularly if his kids are grown and gone, he may confess to his wife. Then they separate, or divorce, or stay together depending on how they both feel about the situation.

"One thing you can be sure of: the man who is intrinsically homosexual and admits this to himself for the first time when he's in a mid-life crisis is going to need all the help he can get. In a gay support group at the Men's Center he'll be able to talk with men who have gone through similar experiences and he can hear how they handled it and how things turned out. I'd say that the support groups for gay men are one of the most valuable services we offer.

"But to get back to your point. I agree that in smaller cities it might be difficult to find enough people to form a support group. Particularly when you realize that it seems to work best when the men don't know or see each other outside of the group. Sometimes church groups will be support groups in small towns, but there's another alternative I think would work better."

"What's that?" I asked.

"It's what's called reevaluation co-counseling. It's a grassroots movement that was started in Seattle by a man named Harvey Jackins. He's written several books; one of his best is called *The Human Situation*. (Rational Island Publishers, Seattle, Washington.)

"The basic premise of reevaluation co-counseling is that every individual wants to do his best. When it comes down to basics there isn't anyone in the world whose goal is to do less than his best. Even a rapist or a thief started out wanting to do the best he could, but somehow he got sidetracked. He just couldn't discover the proper path for himself.

"You'd have to read Jackins's books to really understand his philosophy, but in practice what happens is that each man finds one or two men who are willing to act as co-counselors with him. The theory is that when any of us is hurt, if we can't express the proper emotion—by crying, for example—the experience is buried and scars us. It's sort of a psychotherapeutic approach to what happens. Even child-hood experiences, if they don't lead to the proper emotional response, will deform our psyche a bit. I know I'm not ex-pressing this very well. We actually give a twelve-week course in reevaluation co-counseling every year and it's difficult to tell you in a few minutes how it works. Basically we try to teach men how to let their emotions loose; bare their souls, I guess.

"Anyway, once you find another man, or perhaps two men, who are willing to be co-counselors with you, you arrange to meet regularly with one or both—separately—for two hours, perhaps once a week. For the first fifty minutes you tell him all that's happened since you last met, all the things that have brought you pain or happiness, and he listens and gives you whatever advice and sympathy he can. Then for ten minutes you talk about anything at all—politics, movies, books, whatever—after which, for the next fifty minutes, he unburdens himself and you do the listening, advising, con-soling. For the final ten minutes you relax by again talking about general matters.

"It's important to follow the timing right to the minute. You have to do that to be fair to each other. And you need the ten minutes in the middle and at the end just to unwind. If you've once learned how to open up and express your deepest feelings, the meeting gets to be a real emotional catharsis."

"It sounds like a session with a psychiatrist," I said.

"Exactly," Pat answered. "Really, it's lay psychotherapy. One big factor in favor of this approach is that it's free. You trade an hour of your time for an hour of your co-counselor's time. Since it is really a form of psychotherapy it's very important that you and your co-counselor not be associated in any other way. You should have the co-counseling relationship only."

"How well does it work?" I asked.

"I can tell you, from experience, that it works very well. I meet with my co-counselor every other week. We met once a week for a year but now every other week seems to be enough. If I didn't have those meetings to look forward to I sometimes wonder if I'd be able to cope. Getting all my problems out in the open is such a relief. We all need this kind of ventilation. I feel sorry for those who don't get it.

"Somehow, I think it's easier for women than for men to talk to each other about problems and their emotional reaction to them. In our culture men are supposed to be the stronger sex. To show signs of weakness is considered unmanly. To take a well-publicized example, look what happened to Muskie when he broke down and cried in front of the press. He had every right to cry; his wife had been verbally abused in a vicious manner. Crying was an appropriate human response. Yet the tears were interpreted as a sign that Muskie was too soft, too chicken-hearted to be president. Nonsense. We need men and women as leaders who don't mind showing their emotional responses. If they're kept bottled up too long, they're likely to cause an explosion.

"If you're acquainted with Chrysalis and the women's groups in Minneapolis, you'll know that they are at least ten or twenty times more active than we are. They have more funding, of course, and so their facilities are better, but I'm convinced that the main reason for their success is that women take to this openness better than men. Culture hasn't made crying a sign of weakness in women. I'm not claiming, of course, that you have to cry to show your emotions. That's just an example that comes immediately to mind.

"I'd like to make a suggestion," Pat said. "Why not come to one of our meetings and see what I'm talking about?"

"Fine," I said, "I'll get there as soon as I can." We said goodbye and I drove back to Litchfield.

A couple of weeks later, on December 22, I went to a meeting of a general-issue support group at the Men's Center. I had asked Pat if they met over the holiday season and he assured me that they did. "In fact, that's one of the loneliest times of the year if you're having emotional or family problems. We never close during the holiday season."

It was a cold night. In Minnesota, when we say cold we mean COLD. It was 27° below zero and the wind chill factor was 63° below zero when I pulled into the parking lot of the old junior high school building that housed the Men's Center.

The facilitator, a man I'll call Matt (all names in this chapter are fictitious), knew I was coming. "Pat told me you might drop in," he said as he introduced himself. "Welcome to the support group. I hope you'll find the experience valuable."

I had arrived at ten minutes before seven, and by seven o'clock there were eight of us in the room. We introduced ourselves, first names only. "I guess it will be just one group tonight," Matt said. "The cold was probably too much for some people." He shut and locked the door and the eight of us went into a partly partitioned space and sat on pillows that were arranged in a circle against the walls.

"Why don't we each make an opening statement," Matt said. "A sort of verbal sign-in. I'll start."

Matt spoke for two or three minutes, telling us how he was

feeling. "I've been down a bit this week," he said. "One of my children went to a party, drank some beer, and his high school hockey coach heard about it. He's suspended for the next two games. He feels bad about that, but I think he really feels worse because he let me down. I've tried to assure him that I still love him, but I guess I couldn't hide my disappointment. I'll get over it and so will he, but it's been tough, particularly with Christmas coming."

Paul, about forty-five, said, "I'm still on unemployment. I've got resumés in at five different advertising agencies and at two public relations firms, but so far I've received only one interview offer. That's not scheduled until January. Everything slows down to a snail's pace over the holidays. I have six weeks of unemployment left; after that, if I don't find a job, I don't know what I'll do."

Marvin, about forty, said, "I had a real bad fight with my wife yesterday. We're not even speaking now. She let one of our kids take my car while I was showering after work. I've told her never to let them use my car unless they've asked me, not her. I was planning to go to the Lions Club meeting last night, but without a car I couldn't make it. Her car's been frozen for two days.

"It seems as if we fight over almost everything these days. Fifteen years we've been married and for fourteen of them we got along fine. Now, all of a sudden, nothing's right anymore. I don't know how much more I can take."

Pete, who could have been anywhere between fifty and sixty, said, "Be thankful you've got a wife and kids. I wish I still had mine. Holidays are hell when you're alone.

"This has been the loneliest week I can remember. I get home from the office, have a couple of drinks and watch the evening news, then open a can of stew or heat up a pizza and sit on my butt in that big house reading magazines or watching sitcoms. What a waste! My wife and kids are only five miles away but they might as well be in India for all the good it does me. She won't talk to me, my daughter's married and has her own family to think about, and the son who's still in school doesn't want any part of me. Why I ever blew it—all for a woman who was just looking for a guy with a few bucks to keep her while she studied pottery making— I'll never know. If I could go back five years and do it all over, you can bet I wouldn't be alone now."

So it went. When my turn came I explained that I was there to get material for a book on the mid-life crisis and assured them that I would, of course, respect their confidences. I had had troubles much like theirs, I added, and still had a lot of problems, but I thought that that evening I'd listen rather than talk. They nodded their acceptance.

Once each of the seven had made an introductory statement, a general conversation began. I won't try to quote it here; I didn't take any notes. What it amounted to was a wide-ranging discussion of the problems of each man. They all had something to say about wives, girl friends, children, jobs, and all the other subjects that came up as they talked. When the subject of children came up one man started talking about his relations with his father and that seemed to trigger a flood of son-father reminiscences and commentaries that lasted half an hour. I found it very difficult not to get into the conversation and tell them about my relations with my father, and how I viewed my relationship with my three sons.

The time went by so quickly that I was startled when the facilitator said, "We'll have to stop now. It's ten minutes of nine, time to sum up." Once again we went around the circle, each man stating briefly what he thought of the night's discussion. At nine o'clock the meeting ended.

It was obvious that everyone had enjoyed the session and had found support among this group of strangers or near strangers. Not only did each of the men say just that, but now each of them seemed buoyant although most of them had had rather a hangdog look when the meeting began. I'm certain that if the facilitator had kept the meeting going everyone would have been delighted to talk for another two or three hours.

As I was putting on my coat I asked Matt about this. "Why not just let everyone keep talking," I said, "it seemed to do them so much good."

Matt smiled. "For one thing," he said, "I have to get up at 7:00 and go to work tomorrow. If I were here until two in the morning, and I could be if we just let this run on, I'd be beat all day.

"Another more important reason is that we've learned by experience that two hours is just about all the time that most groups can comfortably take. As I'm sure you noticed, it's a very intense experience for some of them. After two hours you feel hyper, but often you're emotionally exhausted. They know that they can come back again next week, so it's not as though we're tossing them out in the cold. Two of the men who were here tonight—Marvin and Peter—have been regulars for over six months. I don't think either of them has missed more than one meeting."

"I would have thought that by now they would have joined a spin-off group," I said.

"As you know, that often happens," Matt said, "but some men prefer to keep coming to the open meetings. They find that they can speak more openly to people they haven't met before. Even if spin-off groups are composed of people who don't see each other outside the group, once the group friendship develops some men find it difficult to be as frank as they once were. In these open meetings no one worries much about how they appear to the others. They can unburden themselves freely."

"Over all, how much good do you think these support groups do?" I asked.

"All I can base my answer on," Matt said, "is the feedback

I get from the participants. Without exception they feel group support has been an enormous help.

"I can also say that just watching them from week to week, in the open groups and in some of the spin-off groups I've helped launch, I can notice a tremendous improvement in attitude and demeanor. Frankly, there have been times when I've wondered if some men who first join aren't actually suicidal. I've even suggested to a few that they seek more formal psychiatric help. All have preferred just to stick with the group and none, I'm happy to say, has ever committed suicide; at least as far as I know, and if they had I'm sure I'd have heard of it."

I said goodbye to Matt and the other men who were still around and left. I didn't go back to any more meetings; I couldn't see that I would learn more by doing so. These weren't structured groups that went from A to B to C in any ordered fashion. They were, as I had known before I attended, loose organizations where men came to get things off their chests and hope for help from other men in stressful situations. I did talk to men who had been active in support groups while going through mid-life crises (one of the facilitators had, at my request, asked them to call me) and, without exception, they told me that attendance at group meetings had been of enormous help to them. "Just talking with others who had been through what I was going through took a lot of the loneliness away," one of them told me. Another said, "The suggestions I got from others in the group encouraged me to take a chance and move to an entirely new job. I don't think I'd have had the courage if I hadn't talked to others who had done it."

To my surprise, about half the men who attended the group were married. "My wife has been marvelous," one man told me, "but there are some things I just couldn't bring myself to talk with her about. One thing, for example, was the sexual attraction I was feeling for my fifteen-year-old daughter. I wouldn't have dared to mention it to her. But in a group, with complete anonymity, I felt safe in bringing it up, though it took me three weeks to do it. Fortunately, we'd gotten to talk about sexuality in general, so it worked out naturally. Two other guys admitted they'd had similar problems and explained that the feeling wasn't totally unnatural, that it was something that would pass. You can't believe how relieved I was to get that worry off my mind. In fact, once I talked it out, the problem just seemed to disappear in about a month."

There is no doubt that for the man in crisis, a support group, if he can find one, may offer important help. I found the Minneapolis group by asking at the Women's Center if such a group existed. In any big city one should be able to get the names and phone numbers of groups by calling mental health centers, university hospitals, YMCAs, YMHAs, or other similar organizations.

In smaller towns, where formal support groups don't exist, it's worth trying the one-on-one co-counseling method. If even that isn't feasible, for one reason or another, then choosing one or two of your friends in whom you can confide may be a satisfactory substitute. I have two friends in Litchfield to whom I feel I can talk very frankly and who offer consolation and advice, whichever is appropriate. I also have one friend on the East Coast, a man who has been a close friend since our medical school days, who has often listened to my tales of woe over the last thirty years. I've done the same for him. We've each spent a fortune on long distance calls, but I'm sure neither of us regrets one dime.

Particularly at crisis time it's important to have one or two male friends to whom you can speak with complete openness. No matter how close we may be to our wives, there are always some subjects it's easier to talk about to another man. To state the obvious, women see things from a female perspective, which is not always the same as the male's. Advice and evaluation from another man can do much to help solve problems of the male mid-life crisis. Whether a man gets that advice from a professional counselor, a support group, a co-counselor, a very close friend, or from all four may depend on his personality and/or his circumstances. But he certainly ought to find another male or males in whom he can confide.

SIX

Dealing with Specific Problems

No matter how much general support the man in crisis receives, or from what source he receives it, he is still going to have to deal with the six major problems that are inevitably part of the mid-life crisis: insomnia, excessive use of alcohol, impotence, marital problems, job dissatisfaction, and fear of ill health and/or death. I list them in no particular order, since the intensity of each symptom may vary from case to case. Let's consider them in the order in which I've listed them.

INSOMNIA

If there is one subject on which, through personal experience, I am a bit of an expert, it is insomnia. As I've said, I am one of those people who decide whether or not they are tired by looking at a clock. If I haven't had at least seven, and preferably eight, hours of sleep in any night, I swear I'm tired the next day.

Insomnia is a very common problem for the man in a mid-life crisis. Any time that one's mind is in a turmoil, it's extremely difficult to get to sleep, and if there is one thing all men in a mid-life crisis suffer from, it's that kind of turmoil.

81

Sometimes the insomnia prevents the man from falling asleep; sometimes it begins when he wakes up after two or three hours of sleep; sometimes it causes him to wake at 4:00 A.M. and just lie there until it's time to get up. One of the most excruciatingly painful types of insomnia is the one that begins at about 4:00 A.M. and then allows the victim to fall asleep for fifteen minutes just before he has to get up to go to work. I suffered from that particular form of insomnia for about three months. I don't know the physiological explanation for it, but I suspect that what happens is that the victim, knowing he'll have to get up soon anyway, stops worrying about getting back to sleep and—*voila!*—he drifts off.

Before we get deeper into insomnia, let me mention another problem, slightly less common but just as devastating, that the man in crisis may develop: hypersomnia. He may toss and turn all night but when it's time to get up and face the day, all he wants to do is crawl back beneath the covers and drift off into a half sleep. He can't stand the idea of going out into the world.

This behavior is typical of those in depression, and the man in crisis is frequently depressed. Shirley, the wife of one man in depression, told me, "It got so that at least three times a week Paul would say, 'Call my boss and tell him I've got the flu' or a migraine or some other ailment—anything just so he didn't have to go to work. I knew his boss couldn't possibly believe me—no one could have as many ailments as Paul claimed to have—but for two months he let Paul get away with it. Paul had worked for the company for twenty years, and he'd always been a good employee.

"Finally, however, he told Paul that he'd better get to a doctor and have a complete physical checkup to make certain some underlying condition wasn't causing all these minor illnesses. That was a break for me, because I'd been trying, without success, to get Paul to see a doctor. Before Paul's visit I called the doctor and told him about all Paul's problems as I saw them. The doctor examined Paul and then referred him to a psychologist. The psychologist got him on the road to recovery."

The man in crisis may have a number of reasons for not wanting to get out of bed. If he has just been passed over for a promotion, in favor of some younger man, just being in the office is a constant reminder of what he sees as his failure. If his job has begun to bore him, the thought of another day of working at it may actually give him a headache. If he has started an affair with some woman at his office, he may not want to be around her because he'll then think about all the ramifications of that liaison. Fundamentally, by staying curled up in his bed, sleeping or just resting, the man in crisis avoids a world he no longer finds pleasant.

When a man in crisis does get to the stage where he's skipping work, staying in bed two or three days a week, then it is certainly time for him to seek medical help. This behavior almost invariably means the man is in a rather severe depression. Psychiatric therapy, counseling and, perhaps as a temporary measure, mood-elevating pills may give him back the emotional strength he needs to fight off all the other problems of the mid-life crisis. Now, back to insomnia.

The key to getting over insomnia is, as you might suspect, to stop worrying about it. But, of course, it's a lot easier to tell yourself you're not going to worry about sleeping than it is to actually put it out of your mind.

There are, fortunately, a number of things you can do to cure yourself of insomnia. Not all of them will help everyone, but some of them will help most people. Here are some of the things that are widely recommended, and a few things that have helped me, which I haven't seen listed elsewhere.

(1) Get some physical exercise at least two or three times a week and every day if possible. I find that on the days I exercise vigorously I always sleep better at night. Before I had my second bypass operation I played racquetball at least

three or four times a week (except during the early weeks of my crisis). Since that operation I've been reluctant to play competitive racquetball since I am one of those people who simply cannot play at anything less than full speed. We don't have an indoor tennis court in Litchfield so tennis is out in the cold weather which, in Minnesota, means about seven months of the year. I could jog, but I find jogging terribly boring and, besides, jogging in very cold weather when you have coronary artery disease is not highly recommended; it can be dangerous. A brisk walk of three or four miles is good exercise, but I find walking as boring as jogging. Swimming would be fine, but the high school pool is available to adults only about twice a week, in the evening, so that won't do.

For me the answer has been an exercise bicycle. That's boring too, I admit, but I've set it up in front of the television set in our basement. In Minnesota the network news goes on at 5:30 in the afternoon and that's when I get on my bike. I peddle during the full half hour of the news, usually going about fifteen miles (according to the meter) and working up a good, heavy sweat. I never used to watch television news— I'm a newspaper person—but I'd never get on that exercise bicycle if I didn't have something I could do besides peddle.

Whatever you do for exercise ought to be done at least two or three hours before you go to bed so you have time to unwind after revving up your body.

(2) Go to bed and get up at the same time every day. Once you hit forty, your body becomes accustomed to certain fixed patterns that are difficult if not impossible to alter. It amazes me to watch the way my kids can flop on a bed or a couch or even a chair at any time of the day or night and sleep as much as sixteen hours at a crack. I remember that I could do that, too, when I was a kid, but once middle age approaches such behavior is out of the question. If you're used to getting up at 7:30 in the morning, it's as if you have a built-in alarm clock which, in a sense, you do. When 7:30

arrives, you wake up, even on weekends when it's not necessary to get up. Once in a while, if you're lucky, you'll be able to drift back to sleep, but most of the time you might as well resign yourself to getting out of bed.

If you're used to going to bed at 11:00, then that's the time you ought to go to bed. That's the time your body is going to be ready for sleep. At 10:30 you won't be tired and by 11:30 you'll be past your optimum go-to-bed time. If you're having insomnia troubles do your damndest to get to bed at the same time each night.

Sleeping is a lot like eating. By the age of forty most of us have established eating patterns. At certain hours of the day, we get hungry. If we don't eat at those times, then our appetites go away. Sleeping follows the same sort of rhythm.

(3) Eat or drink something (non-alcoholic) just before you go to bed. You've probably noticed that you get tired right after you've eaten a meal. I know that if I don't have a chance to lie down for twenty minutes after lunch, I'm half asleep for an hour or two. That's why so many people drink coffee after meals; the caffeine counteracts the natural drowsiness that eating induces. It's an unnatural way to stay awake but in our society, where siestas are out of the question for most people, we have to resort to unnatural methods to keep functioning.

(Lyndon Johnson used to take an after-lunch nap whenever possible. A reporter once asked him if he just laid down in his clothes or if he put on his pajamas. Johnson supposedly replied, "I always put on my jammies and when I do my jammies say to me, 'Lyndon, you go to sleep.' " I believe it.)

The reason you get tired after eating is that digestion requires an increase in the blood flow to the stomach and intestine. More blood for the digestive system means less blood to the brain, and less blood to the brain means less cerebral activity. That's why it makes sense to eat something just before retiring.

It should be something light. A heavy meal may get your digestive system churning and that will keep you awake. A glass of milk and a slice of toast, or a small dish of ice cream or even half a bowl of breakfast cereal is about right. Supposedly foods with tryptophan (a protein) in them are particularly effective. (Tryptophan is supposed to be a sort of natural sleeping pill.) Milk and beef both contain tryptophan. Personally, I've never noticed that it makes much difference what you eat, as long as you eat something. (Obvious exceptions, for adults, are such things as pizza or raw onions, which will cause heartburn in almost everyone over the age of thirty-five.)

(4) Make sure that the room in which you sleep is very dark. I was absolutely amazed to find how much better I was able to sleep after Joan bought very dark curtains for our bedroom. I hadn't realized how much the light coming through our thin curtains contributed to my inability to sleep. Let me assure you, if your bedroom isn't dark now, you're going to be delighted at how much heavy drapes contribute to your slumber.

(5) This is so obvious I'm almost embarrassed to mention it, but I know it is frequently overlooked: make certain that your bed and pillow(s) are comfortable.

Personally, I hate those pillows that are filled with some sort of light, synthetic material. I like a good heavy pillow stuffed with feathers. They're tough to find, in some areas, but for me they're well worth looking for. I have a friend in Massachusetts, about my age, and he and his wife drove out to see us a couple of summers ago. When they were unpacking the car the first thing he took out was his pillow; he'd carted it with him all across the country, bringing it into the bedroom of each motel at which they stayed. Very smart man.

As far as mattresses are concerned, I know that a lot of "authorities" claim that a stiff mattress is good for one's back, but I prefer a nice soft mattress and a spring with a lot of give to it. That's the kind of bed in which I'm most comfortable.

I also need a king-size bed, if I'm not in the bed alone. I toss around a lot and even a queen-size bed is too confining. It's amazing how much my sleeping improved when, twenty years ago, Joan and I got rid of the three-quarter-size double bed we'd had since we first got married. The king-size bed added at least one hour a night to my sleep.

If you're having trouble with insomnia, go to your local furniture store and try out the beds, mattresses, and pillows. You may be surprised at what a difference a bed change will make.

(6) Every spring, when Joan and I move from our home in town to our lake cabin, I'm delighted to find I can sleep an extra half hour in the morning. I shouldn't be surprised, since it's happened every year for the last ten years, but over the winter I tend to forget how quiet it is at the lake. Litchfield is hardly what a city dweller would call a noisy place, but still, beginning at about six in the morning, cars start moving along our residential street. That doesn't happen at the lake, and the extra quiet, I'm sure, is responsible for my extra sleep. If you live in a big city you may not be able to get away from noise as completely as we do, but it might be possible to shift from a front bedroom to a back bedroom. Put the kids in the noisy part of the house; kids can sleep through anything.

Conversely, if your insomnia is the kind that prevents you from falling asleep when you first go to bed, you might try putting a radio near the head of the bed and turning it on when you go to bed. If you're listening to the radio then it's difficult to think about things like college tuitions, death, and taxes.

The trick is to find a station that plays the sort of thing to which you only have to half listen. We have a station that plays Mantovani-type music all night, and that works well for me. Even a baseball or basketball game, when you don't really care who wins, will do nicely. I've tried listening to a jazz station, but for me that's no good; when I listen to jazz I really listen.

Why should absolute quiet help some people sleep, while background noise (or music) helps others? For the same reason psychologists use peace and quiet to induce hypnosis in some patients and use distracting lights and sounds to induce hypnosis in other patients. Which will work best on a given patient must be determined by trial and error.

(7) This next may sound crazy, but let me assure you that it really helped me: I never, never look at my watch once I've gone to bed.

I used to look at it all the time. I'd drift off at midnight, wake up and look at my watch, and say, "Wow, it's two o'clock; I've got five more hours to sleep. That's great." I'd go back to sleep and when I woke up again I'd look at my watch and say, "Damn. It's almost five. I'd better hurry and get back to sleep; only two hours left." Naturally, worrying about how quickly I could get back to sleep would keep me awake.

Now that I never look at my watch I always assume I have plenty of time to sleep, so I'm relaxed and, consequently, can get back to sleep easier. It's a little thing but, believe me, it helps.

(8) This might actually be the most important factor in combatting insomnia: when you go to bed, remind yourself that no matter how much or little sleep you get you're going to be fine the next day. I'm not kidding; you *will* be fine. Even if you sleep only two hours, if you're in bed for five or six hours you're going to get plenty of rest. All kinds of tests have been done that have proven, over and over again, that two or three nights or even a week of only two or three hours of sleep have absolutely no detrimental effect on mechanical or intellectual performance. If you have a big business deal coming up, or if you're playing for the local tennis cham-

pionship, you'll be perfectly all right with a minimal amount of sleep. So forget about your "need" to sleep. It isn't a "need" at all.

(9) I've saved sleeping pills for last because that's exactly when they should be used—last. Once in a great while it's all right to take a sleeping pill. Let's say there's been a death in the family or you're due to have a confrontation with your boss the next morning—such things can understandably keep you awake and fretting most of the night. So take a pill.

But be sure it's the right pill. We've learned a great deal about sleeping pills in the last few years and there are a lot of new ones on the market. Your doctor has plenty to choose from but he may be one of those doctors who don't keep up with what's new in the pharmaceutical world. To be safe, ask him some questions about the pill.

If it's just a one- or two-night situation, then your major concern need only be hangover; ask your doctor how long the effect of the pill lasts. Some pills will cause drowsiness for as long as twelve hours. You won't want one of those if you're going to meet your boss in the early morning.

If you need sleeping pills for a couple of weeks—if one of your family has a lingering illness, for example, or if you're in for a long, drawn-out tax audit—ask for a pill that doesn't interfere with R.E.M. (rapid eye movement) sleep. A pill that does inhibit R.E.M. sleep blocks dreaming or, at the most, allows very few dreams. Nembutal, seconal—all the barbiturates—block R.E.M. sleep. If you take an R.E.M. blocker you may have a rebound, with more dreams than you want, when you quit them.

This dream rebound can be very disturbing. Your sleep becomes, or so it seems, one constant series of dreams or nightmares—not a very pleasant way to spend a night.

(One of the explanations for the hallucinations that are often part of delirium tremens, the "D.T.'s," during which an alcoholic thinks he sees pink elephants, rats, and other terrifying sights, is that the alcoholic has for so long depressed his R.E.M. sleep by using alcohol that now the dreams and nightmares he should have been having during previous nights surface during his waking as well as his sleeping hours.)

Remember that all sleeping pills lose their effectiveness eventually. Some of the new ones, such as Dalmane and Restoril, will remain effective for a month or more, but for most patients the barbiturates lose their effectiveness after a week or two. If you've been taking one seconal a night for three weeks, and you swear it's still effective, I can assure you that you might as well be taking a placebo; the effectiveness is only due to the fact that you believe the pill is effective. After three weeks of use you'll have to increase the dose substantially to get any real effect.

Remember that the brain's response to sleeping pills, and to all drugs, is to a certain extent unpredictable. I've known patients who weigh 110 pounds who need two 100-milligram seconals to get to sleep, and I've known patients who weigh 240 pounds who are knocked out for six hours if they take one 50-milligram seconal.

Finally, I've found that one or two aspirin at bedtime often serve as a very effective sleeping pill. Once you hit middle age one of the things that help keep you awake, or wake you after you've been sleeping for a few hours, are aches and pains in your muscles and joints. And then there's also the discomfort that develops as your bladder fills while you're sleeping. Aspirin diminishes these minor disturbances and may help you get a better night's sleep. I've found it works very well for me.

One way the male in mid-life crisis should *not* treat insomnia is with alcohol. Alcohol is certainly the least effective sleep producer you can find. There's no question that a few hefty belts before going to bed will help you fall asleep quickly—dreamless sleep, by the way, because alcohol blocks

R.E.M. sleep. It's also certain that three or four hours later you're going to wake up and, in all probability, stay awake. When the effect of the alcohol wears off, the brain becomes not only active, but hyperactive. Anyone who has ever had too much to drink will testify that one thing you cannot do with a hangover is sleep. You'll be far better rested if you've slept two or three hours in a night without any booze than if you've slept four or five hours after drugging yourself with alcohol.

Which brings us to a second major problem of the mid-life crisis: alcohol abuse.

ALCOHOL

I like alcohol. In fact, to be right up front with my prejudices, I'm sort of wary of people who don't drink at all—except, of course, for reformed alcoholics. Personally, I think alcohol is one of life's pleasures and there aren't so many pleasures around that we can afford to pass one up.

I'm also afraid of alcohol. The Nolen family history is not particularly encouraging where booze is concerned. I had a grand-uncle who was pickled for a large part of his adult life, and my father didn't handle alcohol well. He used to say, "One drink makes me feel like a new man, but then the new man wants a drink." He was a smart man and he recognized his weakness. He was one of those for whom "one drink was too many and a hundred weren't enough," so for most of his life he abstained. But when he drank, perhaps half a dozen times a year, he got drunk. Not sloppy, incoherent, falling over drunk, but drunk enough so he'd behave like an ass. My mother absolutely dreaded seeing my father take a drink. She knew that, for him, one drink spelled trouble.

My tolerance for alcohol is far greater than my father's was. I never took a drink until I was twenty-five and a senior in medical school; my mother was afraid I'd be like my father, so I abstained for her sake. Besides, I didn't really miss it. I started drinking when I was twenty-five because it was then that I developed hypertension. In those days—that was 1953— there weren't any medications that effectively lowered blood pressure, so the doctor who first discovered I was hypertensive suggested I take a little phenobarbital when I thought I was going to be under stress. I decided that if I was going to take something to relax I would prefer alcohol to phenobarbital because alcohol seemed likely to be more fun. So I started drinking. I still remember my first drink—whiskey and Coca-Cola—a concoction I wouldn't think of drinking now.

I drank off and on—not really very much, in retrospect— between 1953 and 1960. Those seven years were my Bellevue years and I never drank when I was on duty, which was usually every other night and weekend, nor did I drink much when I was off duty. I was just too tired. All I wanted to do on my nights off was visit with Joan, play with the kids, eat, and go to bed.

I started drinking more when I went into practice and, by the time I hit forty-five, I was having two or three scotches-and-soda just about every night. It was a bad habit but it was what all our friends in our age group were doing.

This rather lengthy preamble about my drinking habits is necessary, I think, so that the reader will understand my perspective when I write about alcohol and the male mid-life crisis. I drink, I like to drink, and I deplore people who drink to excess, but I've done it myself more often than I like to remember.

I am also very skeptical when it comes to the diagnosis of alcoholism. I realize that alcoholism is a dangerous, sometimes lethal, disease; you don't spend five years at Bellevue Hospital without becoming acutely aware of the ravages of alcoholism. I do, however, think that many, perhaps even most, of the counselors in the field of alcoholism tend to overdiagnose the condition. When anyone comes to them for advice they assume that person is an alcoholic and it's very difficult to convince them otherwise. Peter, a friend of mine whom I know very, very well and who I know is not an alcoholic, had an accident one evening after he had been drinking. The judge insisted he see a counselor at a clinic for alcoholics. "The guy asked me if I ever drank at noon, and I said, 'No,' " Peter later told me. " 'Ah ha!' the counselor said, 'afraid to drink at noon, eh? That's a sign of the true alcoholic.'

"The next day I saw him again and I guess he'd forgotten who I was because he asked me again if I ever drank at noon. This time I said, 'Very, very rarely. Maybe one martini if I'm entertaining a customer at lunch.' 'Ah, ha!' the guy says again. 'Can't even have lunch without a drink, can you? That's a pretty certain sign of a true alcoholic.' I decided I just couldn't win."

What bothers me about those who counsel alcoholics is that most of them seem to take the attitude, "Look, you're an alcoholic. Let's treat that," without ever digging deeply enough into the victim's personal life to discover why he became an alcoholic. Admittedly there are people who are alcoholics from the moment they take their first drink; once they've tried alcohol, they can never stay away from it. I suspect, however, that such people are much fewer in number than the general literature would lead us to believe. I think that if the counselor dug hard enough he'd find the problem that triggered the uncontrolled drinking.

I know that's the case with the typical man in mid-life crisis. Until the age of forty (or so) he has been able to drink moderately. Now, suddenly, he goes into crisis and finds he cannot control his drinking. His wife, or his boss, or a friend persuades him to go to an alcohol counselor and he is told he is now an alcoholic and will never be able to drink moderately again. This is a devastating blow to a man who heretofore has enjoyed the camaraderie of a few beers with his friends on appropriate occasions. He's already depressed and this depresses him even more.

Worse, I think that in most cases it's a lie. This man is not an alcoholic in the sense that he has suddenly acquired the disease, alcoholism. He is, rather, a reactive alcoholic; he overdrinks in reaction to the mid-life crisis that has over-whelmed him. Once the crisis ends (as—I repeat—crises al-most invariably do) he may well be able to resume social drinking. The reactive alcoholic can be compared to the pa-tient with reactive depression, precipitated perhaps by a death in the family. Once the cause of the depression is far enough behind him, the patient with reactive depression gets better. The person with the illness we call alcoholism, however, is like the patient with intrinsic depression. It's a real disease, not one triggered by external events.

It's neither fair nor true to tell the man in crisis who starts to drink without control that he is an alcoholic who will never again be able to touch alcohol. What he should be told is that for the time being, as long as he is in crisis, he should keep away from alcohol because, under stress, its effects are likely to be greater than is usual. Later, when his crisis is over, he may well be able to go back to his customary social drinking. But it's easier just to say to the man, "No alcohol, ever again," and that, unfortunately, is just what most coun-selors do.

When I mentioned my theory to a close friend, Brad, a man who had admittedly been an alcoholic (he used to drink a pint of whiskey and six or eight cans of ale regularly to help him get to sleep), he said,"You say anything like that down at Saint Margaret's (fictitious name), and they'll lock you up. The doctors down there say, 'Alcoholism is a primary disease! Just like cancer. Don't give us any business about it being a reaction to anything else.' It makes them furious when anyone says anything to the contrary."

"How about you?" I asked. "You've been through their program, haven't you?"

"Sure have," Brad said, "three times."

"Do you agree with me that at least in some patients the alcohol dependency is transient, a reaction to some circumstance in life?"

"Hell, yes," Brad said. "No question about that, in my opinion. But I'd never say so to those guys at Saint Margaret's. They'd go wild.

"Their whole policy is to treat alcoholics like scum anyway. Make them feel as if they aren't worth a damn until they're completely off the booze. They claim that taking a tough line is the only way to cure anyone."

Having said all this, let me now say that alcohol is a serious problem for the male in crisis. Whatever other problems he has are going to be compounded by alcohol. Sometimes impotent? Alcohol may make you impotent all the time. Inclined to chase young women? Alcohol will turn you into a repulsive satyr. Grouchy with the wife and children? Alcohol will make you an ogre. Alcohol is bad, bad, bad for the man in crisis.

As Rust Hills wrote, in his wonderfully funny and sadly neglected book, *How To Do Things Right*, everyone wants to cut down on his drinking but no one wants to quit drinking. How true. As a person who drinks let me say that I don't think the male in crisis has to quit drinking. If he tries to do so, especially at crisis time, he is almost certainly going to fail. And another failure, at a time when his whole life may seem to him a failure, is something he definitely does not need.

The male at mid-life does need to realize that his tolerance for alcohol is certainly not what it was when he was twenty-five years old. As we age, our brain cells don't require nearly as much sedation to knock them out as they did when we were younger. That, of course, is the way alcohol works: it knocks out the cells in our cerebral cortex, where our good judgment lies and frees our inhibitions. That's why it's fun to get a bit tight. You say and do things that your good judgment wouldn't let you do under ordinary circumstances. It's kind of a pleasant experience, as anyone who has ever had a few drinks will testify. As a friend of mine often says, "I'm going to have a couple of drinks and really *be* someone."

But while you could, perhaps, handle five or six highballs or even ten or twelve beers when you were younger, now two or three highballs or four or five beers are all it takes to release your inhibitions. Drink any more than that and all your rational faculties disappear. You may even knock out your balance center so that you start to stumble. A half dozen highballs may once have made you eloquent (or at least, so it seemed), but now the same amount of alcohol makes your speech slurred or even incoherent. The guy who used to be witty and funny after half a dozen drinks is now a silly, drooling bore. If you don't want that to happen to you, cut back on your alcohol intake as you get older.

Particularly at crisis time. Anyone who has ever had a drink knows that under certain circumstances you can drink more, without getting drunk, than you can under other circumstances. I'm not talking about physical circumstances; it's well known, for example, that if you get some food into your stomach it will take more alcohol to get you drunk than if you drink on an empty stomach. That's a fact with a simple, solid, scientific explanation: you absorb alcohol faster from an empty stomach than you do when your stomach is full of food. I'm talking about psychological circumstances. Let's say you're sitting quietly at home with three or four friends and you decide to have a few drinks. Chances are those drinks won't affect you as quickly or to the same degree as if you were to drink them at a wild party, surrounded by a dozen or so people who are half inebriated. I don't know why that is, and neither does anyone else, as far as I can determine, but it's true.

Just as it's true that if you drink when you're jovial the alcohol will probably increase your elation; if you drink when you're a bit down the alcohol will make you depressed. Since the man in mid-life crisis is almost invariably either in a depression or on the edge of one, alcohol is likely to make him extremely depressed or even despondent. For the mid-life crisis man alcohol is more dangerous than almost any other substance.

The answer is to either stop drinking or to cut down on drinking, and since the first is terribly difficult it's safer to try the second. Innumerable techniques can be used but, as is true whenever you find a problem with many alternative solutions, none of them works every time. Here are some of the methods I've known to be successful.

First, if you're a cocktail drinker switch to highballs. I know that, scientifically speaking, the effects of drinking depend entirely on the amount of alcohol in the drink and not the form in which it comes. I also know, from personal experience and from observing and talking to friends, that the martini is the most dangerous drink known to humankind, and I don't care about alcoholic content. In fact, another physician-writer, the late Dr. Walter Alvarez, devoted one of his widely syndicated medical columns to the ten rules for maintaining harmony between husband and wife. Of the ten rules five were the same one, reiterated: "Never drink martinis." For the male in mid-life crisis, they are lethal.

It's often been said that there's no point in switching from spirits to beer or wine, since it's only the alcohol content that matters. Again, that's scientifically true but practically false. Of course, you can get drunk on beer or wine, but it takes a lot more perseverance to do it that way than to do it with scotch, gin, or bourbon. Personally, when I drink beer

I usually get so bloated after three or four beers that I can't keep drinking the stuff fast enough or long enough to get drunk. With wine, I just get tired of it before it can get me tight. Switching from booze to beer or wine is a good idea. (Warning: beware of the tendency to say, after three or four beers, "I've had enough of that stuff; give me a real drink." If you do that, all is lost.)

Everyone who drinks fairly regularly usually does so at a certain time of day, often between 5:30 and 7:30 in the evening. If that's your practice, then find something else to do between 5:30 and 6:30; take a walk, work later at the office, perhaps do as I do and ride an exercise bicycle. If you keep the dinner hour set at 7:30 you'll have cut your drinking time in half and, unless you cheat by speeding up your pace, your daily alcohol intake will also be cut in half. I've found this a very effective technique for cutting alcohol intake. I've used it successfully to treat not only men in mid-life crises but women and men who are trying to lose weight.

If you're an after-dinner drinker then you're going to have to get out more until you've broken your drinking habit. Movies are great for the after-dinner hours; there's no alcohol available in a movie theater. The movie also gives the mid-life crisis man something to think about other than himself, at least for a few hours. If there aren't a lot of theaters where you live (and there's only one in Litchfield), a long walk after dinner will keep you away from drinking. But I don't have to give you specific advice; the point is, you have to alter the pattern of your life if you're going to change your drinking habits.

If party drinking is your problem you might try arriving a couple of hours late or perhaps even skipping the party entirely. As I think back over the hundreds of parties to which Joan and I have gone in our lives together, fewer than a dozen were really memorable. As far as the rest of them are concerned, I'd have had a better time reading a book, going to a movie, or even watching television. We go to parties thinking, "Maybe this one will be different. Maybe it will really be fun, something we wouldn't want to miss." The odds against most parties being "something we wouldn't want to miss" are so overwhelming as to make the possibility of picking the Irish Sweepstakes winner look like a sure thing. Skip parties and avoid the possibility of getting inebriated; you won't miss a thing.

After I hit fifty-four I found that even two drinks before dinner ruined the rest of my evening. As soon as I finished eating I'd get so sleepy that if I read I could hardly retain any of it. All I could do was watch television, and I've never been much of a TV fan.

Perhaps if I had been able to drink coffee after dinner I would have been able to stay alert, but I couldn't. Caffeine and I don't get along. Not only does it tend to make me tense, but it also makes my heart skip beats. When that happens, I get very nervous. I envy people who can sit and relax and have two drinks before dinner, and a productive evening afterward, but I'm not one of them.

Sometimes, when I'd had two or three drinks before dinner, I'd feel so tired after dinner that I'd go right to bed. I'd be asleep by 9:30 or 10:00. Then, naturally I'd wake up about 3:00 or 4:00 and have trouble getting back to sleep. I refused to take anything to help me sleep—I wasn't going to get hooked on pills again—so I'd just lie there and rest, which wasn't much fun.

Finally I decided the best way to avoid those problems was just not to drink. So I quit. Not entirely; when we go out to a party, or occasionally on a Friday or Saturday night when we're home and I have nothing pressing to do the next day, I'll have a few drinks. However, I used to have drinks six or seven nights a week and now I drink only once or twice a week.

Frankly, it's the smartest move I've made in a long time.

Now, since I'm not tired after dinner, I can sit up and read until midnight and retain what I read. When I go to bed I sleep through the night. At fifty-five I've added an extra three profitable and enjoyable hours to my day. As the song goes, "The days grow short when you reach November," but by cutting out the booze I've added more daylight to those days.

This isn't a book on the dangers of alcoholism. The reason I've spent so much time on alcohol is, to reiterate, that the male in mid-life crisis is highly likely to think he can find an answer to his problems in a bottle. Sure, alcohol will give him temporary release from anxiety, but it will inevitably compound all the other problems that are part of crisis time. One problem alcohol immediately makes worse is impotence, a condition that is so prevalent among men in crisis as to be almost universal.

IMPOTENCE

Perhaps the most distressing of all the problems with which the man in mid-life crisis must deal is impotence. Men fear few things more than impotence: death, perhaps, but I wouldn't bet much money on it. I have heard more than one man say, "I'd rather be dead than impotent." A lot of men are convinced that if they can't have an erection they are not really men at all.

(Perhaps I'd better define impotence. According to Masters and Johnson, impotence is the inability to achieve an erection of sufficient size and stiffness to allow penetration and intercourse more than once in four attempts. In other words, if you fail three out of four times you are considered impotent.)

One of the most prevalent myths of the eighties is that the man in mid-life can and ought to be as sexually active as the man of twenty-five. This is utter nonsense. As a man gets older the frequency and firmness of his erections diminish, and the refractory time—the time it takes him to develop a second erection after he has once had intercourse—grows longer. At twenty-five a man may well be capable of having intercourse five times in a night. The man of forty-five or fifty who can have intercourse two or three times a night, two nights in succession, is a very unusual person.

What is more, the man of forty-five or fifty who has intercourse two or three times a night is pushing himself. At twenty-five his libido might be such that he really wants intercourse four or five times a night. At forty-five or fifty he's simply playing games. In at least 95 percent of cases once—at most twice—is all the sex a man wants. Once at bedtime, perhaps, and if there's time in the morning for relaxed foreplay, perhaps he'll enjoy intercourse again. But the libido diminishes, just as potency does, with age.

At crisis time the male has dozens of concerns other than sex. Not only does he have the financial problems (tuitions, income tax, car payments, etc.) but he has health concerns. He may be worried about the condition of his heart, about the possibility that he has cancer, about losing his teeth or his hair. With all those things on his mind, is it any wonder he can't concentrate on sex?

Still, he tries, because he thinks if he doesn't he isn't being manly. Naturally, once in a while he fails. I would say, and this can't be documented because people won't own up to it, that virtually every male over the age of forty has, on at least one occasion, found himself impotent. Men don't talk about those episodes; neither do their wives or girl friends. They tuck those memories far away in the back of their minds. Sometimes that works, but often, just before the next attempt at intercourse, that memory sneaks to the front of the brain and the man finds himself thinking, "Gee, I hope I'm not going to be impotent again." Worrying about whether you can "do it" almost ensures you'll be a failure. When that happens, it's sad. There's a very wise saying that goes, "Anxiety is the first time you can't do it twice. Panic is the second time you can't do it once."

The man in crisis is almost inevitably going to have impotence problems. If he behaves like most men, he isn't going to discuss his problem. He'll just let it lie there, like his limp penis. He thinks if he doesn't say anything about it, it will go away.

Usually—and unfortunately—his wife won't say anything about it either. This is understandable, the first time it happens. His wife doesn't want to mention his "failure" because she doesn't want her partner to think that it is of major importance to her. If he discusses it, which he probably won't, she'll probably simply reassure him that this was certainly just a fluke, and he'll be fine next time.

But if the next time—and the time after that—he remains impotent, if he doesn't mention it, she certainly should. Sadly, sex counselors tell me that they often see couples with whom male impotence has been a problem for as long as two or three years, and neither husband nor wife has ever mentioned it. Neither one wanted to upset the other, so they pretended there wasn't any problem.

Sad, isn't it?

If a man has been impotent on two or three successive attempts, then he has a problem, and the very first thing he ought to do is mention it to his wife. If he doesn't mention it, she ought to. Gently, of course. Not, "Hey, how come you can't get it up anymore? Don't you love me?" That sort of approach, along with being cruel, is only going to make matters worse. He might say, "Gee, I guess I'm too distracted tonight. Do you mind if we just lie here, hold on to each other, and talk." Women often would just as soon lie with their lovers and talk. They may well prefer it to intercourse and enjoy it as much at certain times.

Talking about an impotence problem may well be enough to solve it. If the male in crisis knows his wife is content to just lie and talk with him, then the pressure to "perform" abates, and when his libido, and hers, returns, the chances are that impotence won't be a problem. Conversation and affection—simple answers to an impotence problem, aren't they? You'd be surprised how infrequently couples use them.

Let's say, however, that conversation, affection, and reassurance don't correct the impotence problem. What next?

We used to say, and a lot of doctors still say, that 90 to 95 percent of impotence cases are psychological in origin. In the last five years doctors have begun to argue that impotence is caused not by psychological factors but by organic factors in about 30 percent of cases. As you might suspect, in many patients impotence comes from two sources. The man who has partial physical or organic impotence, and discovers he can't get satisfactory erections as often as he'd like, begins to worry about this problem, and the worry may shift him from the partial to the total failure category. In any case, when impotence doesn't respond to support and understanding, then it's time to see a doctor who has a special interest in impotence problems.

What are the organic causes of impotence? Number one is long-term diabetes. About half the men who have had diabetes for twenty years or more become impotent. Presumably this is due to arteriosclerotic changes in the blood vessels and to neuritis, both of which often develop in men who have been diabetics for many years.

Impotence may also be caused by hormone deficiencies. Some doctors claim that in as many as 30 percent of patients with impotence it's possible to discover hormone deficiencies or imbalances, most of which can be cured rather easily by hormone shots. These doctors have reported cases in which impotent patients had been treated with psychotherapy for several years without any success, only to improve dramatically—in fact return to normal potency—two weeks after a hormone shot. Whether or not a doctor agrees that hormone

problems contribute to impotence in 30 percent of cases, the
blood test for hormone levels is relatively simple and inex-
pensive and it ought to be done on any impotent man.

Another possible cause of impotence is poor blood supply
to the penis. In order for a penis to become turgid and erect,
blood must flow into it. If the arteries that bring blood to
the penis are completely or partially blocked, they're going
to interfere with erection. There are both direct and indirect
tests that will determine whether enough blood is reaching
the penis. If not, often the blood supply can be improved
with blood vessel surgery.

Paraplegia, multiple sclerosis, and some other rare neu-
rological disorders may also make a man impotent. There
have to be properly functioning nerves going to that penis if
it is going to become erect.

Probably the major cause of organic impotence, aside from
diabetes, is blood pressure medication. Even though impotence is not listed as a possible side effect in every instance,
I can assure you that there is absolutely no blood pressure
medicine which doesn't cause partial or complete impotence
in some of the patients who take it. I've discussed this with
dozens of doctors and haven't yet found a doctor who doesn't
agree. I include in this group even the diuretics, the "water-
losing" pills, such as Diuril or Hydrodiuril. Some blood pressure pills are worse than others; most of the doctors I know
have given up prescribing Aldomet, since impotence is such
a common side effect. A pill that works just fine for one
patient may cause total impotence in another, and vice versa.
Sometimes it's dose related. Smaller doses are well tolerated,
bigger doses produce impotence. There is, however, one saving grace. There are now enough blood pressure pills around
so that if one pill or a combination of pills makes you impotent, your doctor ought to be able to change your prescription and get you onto something that will keep your

blood pressure normal while leaving you potent.

Often, patients on blood pressure pills don't even realize they have become impotent. Along with diminished potency the pill may produce a loss of libido, so the patient thinks, "I'm just getting older; that's why sex doesn't interest me." Not true at all. It's the pills that are causing his loss of sex drive.

Your doctor may not warn you about the impotence-inducing potential of your blood pressure pills. He's afraid if he does so he may make you psychologically impotent. So if your sex drive changes when you go on blood pressure medicines be sure to tell your doctor.

Before concluding that a patient who is impotent has physical or organic impotence, it is customary to do what is called a nocturnal penile tumescense, or N.P.T., test. In this test a gauge is wrapped around the patient's penis when he goes to bed. The gauge is attached to a recording device. If the patient develops an erection while he's sleeping, the attendant will know this is happening and can even look at the erection to see if it appears to be adequate for penetration and intercourse. Men of middle age and older normally have three or four erections a night. Even at sixty-five the average man's penis is erect about an hour and a half every night. The man isn't aware of this, of course, because he's sleeping. A patient who has at least two satisfactory erections a night does not have organic impotence. His impotence is psychological. If he has no nocturnal erections, he has organic impotence.

There is one exception to the N.P.T. test. Occasionally an older man who has abstained from intercourse for a year or more—because, perhaps, his wife has a chronic illness—will get involved with another woman after his wife's death. He attempts to have intercourse and fails. All his hormone and blood vessel tests are normal, but his N.P.T. test shows no erections. He may have what is known as widower's syndrome, an example of what is sometimes called the "use it or lose it" phenomenon.

Such a man may, by using masturbation, achieve orgasm and after a few weeks of intermittent masturbation his N.P.T. test will return to normal. The widower's syndrome, however, is relatively rare. Usually a flat N.P.T. means organic impotence.

For the man with organic impotence, all is not lost. In the last ten years very satisfactory penile prostheses have been developed and thousands of them have been successfully implanted in patients with organic impotence.

The operation is fairly simple. Two rods (they may be rigid, semirigid, or inflatable) are inserted into the corpora—the channels of tiny vessels that run side by side in the penis. The inflatable prostheses are pumped up by a small hand pump that is placed in the scrotum. The rigid prosthesis is always rigid and in position for intercourse; the semirigid can be bent into any satisfactory position. All can be easily and successfully used to have intercourse. Satisfaction rates run between 90 and 95 percent, according to the males who have had prostheses implanted and the females with whom they have had sexual intercourse. Men with implanted prostheses have even fathered children.

I asked one surgeon, who had put in hundreds of these prostheses, whether he would recommend a prosthesis for a patient who had successful intercourse about once in four or five attempts. "That's entirely up to him," the surgeon said. "This is an elective operation. If he's happy with once in five times, or even once in ten times, that's fine with me. Patients vary. I never push anyone to have a prosthesis. All I can say is that those who have had them inserted are almost universally pleased with the results."

The chances are that the average man in mid-life crisis,

with potency problems, does not need a prosthesis. I mention this solution only so the reader will know that even in a "worst case" situation there is an answer to impotence.

A lot of men with impotence problems are understandably reluctant to submit to surgery. They feel as if having a prosthesis inserted is, in a way, cheating. They wonder if there isn't some pill or injection that will restore their potency.

Most doctors will say no. If the patient's hormone levels are normal, then there is nothing to be gained by giving him an injection of the male hormone, testosterone.

I am no longer convinced that this is true. We know, for example, that blood pressure medicines frequently cause impotence, but we don't know precisely why. Perhaps it's because of the effect the blood pressure medicine has on the brain. Maybe a normal level of testosterone isn't enough to stimulate potency when the patient is on other medicines. Whatever the explanation—even though scientifically controlled studies that prove hormone injections will improve potency haven't been done—there are enough reports to make one wonder if, at least in some patients, it isn't worthwhile, despite normal blood hormone levels, to try supplemental testosterone when impotence develops. I believe these injections frequently help.

When I first moved to Litchfield, Harold Wilmot, my senior partner and a good storyteller, told me a story about testosterone. Harold stopped in one of the local coffee shops one morning and, as he was leaving, one of his patients, Tom Rice, a man of fifty, stopped him and said, "Doc, will you do me a favor? I'm going up north to my cabin this morning and I'm going to meet a girl friend from Minneapolis there. I want to be in top shape. Can you fix me up?"

"Sure," Harold said. "Stop down at my office. I'll call Ellen, my office nurse, and tell her to give you a shot."

"Gee, thanks, Doc," Tom said. "I owe you one."

Harold called Ellen, told her what to do, and when he came to the office that afternoon he asked Helen if Tom Rice had stopped in.

"He sure did," Ellen said, "and I did what you said. I gave him 100,000 units of testosterone."

Harold jumped. "A hundred thousand!" he said. "I said ten thousand."

"Gee, I'm sorry," Ellen said. "I must have misunderstood you."

Harold got right on the telephone, called one of Tom's friends and got the phone number of his cabin. After the second ring, Tom answered.

"Tom," Harold said, "how are you doing?"

"Great, Doc, just great," Tom answered. "Three times already."

Harold breathed a sigh of relief. "Wonderful, Tom," Harold said, "how's the girl?"

"Oh," Tom said, "she hasn't arrived yet."

This story, obviously apocryphal, does illustrate how a lot of men, many doctors included, think of testosterone, the sex hormone.

I've had one experience with testosterone therapy that strongly impressed me.

A patient whom I'll call Larry, a fifty-five-year-old construction worker, was having impotence problems. His wife, May, was the person who told me. She called me at my office one afternoon and said, "Doc, poor Larry's having a terrible time. He just can't get it up anymore. He still reads girlie books when he goes to bed, but it doesn't do any good. His thing is just like a rag. I really feel sorry for him."

This sort of reaction from a wife is not untypical. In fact, except that May is more outspoken than many women, I'd say her attitude, as the fifty-two-year-old wife of a man to whom she has been married for twenty-eight years, is almost the rule. May really didn't mind, for herself, the fact that

Larry was impotent. When it came to sex, she still enjoyed it but it was no longer very important to her. What was important to her was Larry's well-being. She knew he wasn't happy, felt less manly, because he couldn't get an erection. "I'm going to get him to come in to see you, Doc. I'll tell him I want him to have a checkup. You ask him about sex. He's too embarrassed to mention it."

This is often the case. In fact, only rarely will a man come directly to me complaining of impotence. Almost invariably it's his wife or girl friend who persuades him to come in.

When Larry came in I examined him completely—there was nothing apparently wrong with either his penis or his testicles—and I managed to bring the subject around to his sex life. He admitted he was having problems. He wasn't on blood pressure pills and he wasn't a heavy drinker. I drew some blood for hormone level measurements and told him to come back in a week.

His hormone levels were normal. We don't do N.P.T. testing in Litchfield but even if he was having nocturnal erections it was certain that he wasn't having erections when he wanted them. Thinking his problem was probably psychological, I decided to give him a shot of normal saline (salt water), a placebo. "This stuff is dynamite," I said as I injected him. "Come back in a couple of weeks and let me know how you're doing."

Two weeks later he returned and I could tell from the expression on his face that he was no better. "Nothing, Doc," he said. "Not even a wiggle. I really feel sorry for May."

"Tell you what, Larry," I said, "I'm going to give you another shot. Sometimes it takes two doses. I'm sure this will do it. Come back in another couple of weeks." I gave him the placebo injection again.

Back he came, still dejected. "Nothing, Doc. For all the good those shots are doing you might as well be giving me water." I cringed a little.

"Okay, Larry," I said, "I'm going to try something different. Let's see how this works." Intentionally I didn't give him the verbal encouragement I had given him when I injected the placebo. This time I gave him 100 milligrams of depotestosterone, a long-acting male hormone.

Two weeks later Larry was all smiles. "That did it, Doc. I'm back to normal. Not like when I was twenty, you know, but a couple of times a week. May's as pleased as she can be."

So was I. I told Larry to come back every three weeks—three weeks is about as long as a shot of depotestosterone lasts. Every six months I'd talk with Larry, and he'd assure me his sex life was fine. I'd also examine his prostate; testosterone doesn't cause cancer of the prostate, but if a patient develops prostate cancer, testosterone will speed its growth. Larry's prostate was fine.

One of the best ways to tell whether a medicine is doing its job is to look at patient compliance. If the patient keeps refilling his prescription or, as in Larry's case, comes in regularly for his shot, then you can be sure the treatment is effective. Larry has been getting his testosterone shot every three weeks for almost three years. That's fairly irrefutable evidence it's working.

As I wrote earlier in this book, what we don't know about brain chemistry is staggering. Perhaps when some men reach mid-life the brain cells that have to do with libido and potency won't respond to what we consider normal testosterone levels. Maybe they need more testosterone stimulation to stir them up. There are all sorts of anecdotal reports of success in treating impotence with testosterone. Ordinarily I discount anecdotal reports, but because of my experience with Larry and a few other patients I think it's worthwhile to try a short course of testosterone injections on a patient with impotence, even if his testosterone blood levels are normal. If it works, he won't mind in the least if you can't explain scientifically why it does.

If testosterone alone doesn't work, you might try to talk your doctor into giving you 100 milligrams of aqueous testosterone together with 5 milligrams of decadron (a cortisone-like drug) and 1,000 micrograms of Vitamin B_{12}. In certain circles this is known as a "sex cocktail." It doesn't make sense, but I know dozens of men, including a couple of M.D.s, who swear it's done wonders for them. Perhaps the increased potency is just a side effect of the feeling of well-being that testosterone and cortisone induce in many patients. So what? If there are no medical reasons why you can't take testosterone or decadron, the sex cocktail may work very nicely for you.

In the last couple of years we've acquired what might be called reverse evidence that testosterone stimulates the libido and the sex drive. Depo-Provera is a hormone that supresses the production of testosterone. It has been offered as optional treatment to criminal sex offenders and those who have agreed to use it have found that their sex drives have, indeed, disappeared. The use of Depo-Provera is called "hormonal castration." The doctors who have had the most experience with it (chiefly those from Johns Hopkins) claim that it works very well. It seems only logical to conclude that if the libido and sex drive can be destroyed by the use of drugs that inhibit testosterone, the reverse would also be true; and this often seems to be the case.

If you're reluctant to take hormone injections, then I think it's reasonable to try to stimulate one's libido with pornography. There's no question that erotic or pornographic literature or pictures will cause arousal in both males and females. Some women may object to their husbands using pornography to stimulate an erection, but in the 1980s that's not as much of a problem as it once was. If a man gets an erection while watching an X-rated film on a videocassette, or while reading the letters or counsel pages of *Penthouse* (pages I invariably find very erotic), he can use that erection to have intercourse with his wife. Often, once he has managed to break the impotence barrier using erotic stimuli, his self-confidence will return and he won't need *Penthouse* anymore. And even if he does, what of it? If the woman in his life loves him, and he loves her, they shouldn't worry about what has to be used to help them enjoy a complete sex life.

For the sake of completeness, let me mention the things that diminish the chances of success in a sexual venture. Alcohol leads the list; the old Shakespearean saw that alcohol increases desire and diminishes performance remains true. A youngster can have sex on eight beers and still perform nicely; a male in mid-life may well wilt if he's had two drinks.

Don't force yourself to indulge in sex. If you don't feel like it, don't try. If you're worrying about a specific business problem, a pain in your chest, whether to buy a new car, forget about sex. At middle age, sex may require your full attention if it's to be successful.

On the other hand, try not to think of it as a challenge. Believe me, most women aren't going to commit suicide if you, their lover, fail to get an erection. They'll be perfectly satisfied with the affection you show them; the affection that is, except in our orgasm-crazy society, the essence of love. If you begin showing affection, and then get an erection, and then have intercourse, fine. If you don't get any erection, fine, too; next time, or the time after, you will. But if you dwell on the lack of an erection, if that possibility is foremost in your mind the next time you take your pants off, it will be a long time between erections.

THE "NEW" WOMAN

As the man in crisis battles his impotence problem, one of the possibilities he is likely to consider is that he is impotent because he is no longer "turned on" by his wife. He may even decide to test this hypothesis. He picks up a prostitute or, more likely in the eighties, takes a woman acquaintance to lunch and, in a shorter or longer period, to bed. He discovers to his delight that with this "new" woman he is not impotent. In fact, for the first time in many years he's up to "doing it" twice in one afternoon. His faith in himself is restored, he feels twenty years younger, and he starts an affair with his "new" woman.

Before long his affair, which began as a relatively innocent test of his potency, has become a love match. He finds that the hours he manages to steal from his family to spend with his girl friend are always pleasant, cheerful, and exciting. While he's with her he doesn't give a thought to the problems he's having with his children, to concerns about needing a new station wagon, to worrying about whether he ought to have the house painted this summer. He's living in a dream world and, because men in crisis rarely think clearly about emotional matters, he may decide that what he really needs to solve all his problems is a new wife. That, he thinks, will make a new man of him. But before he makes such a radical decision, he had better give this matter plenty of thought.

For example, one thing the man in crisis tends to forget, as he carries on his affair with the new woman, is that over all the years he and his wife have been married they have shared many experiences that will tie them together for the rest of their lives.

Children, for example. When I was in my early thirties, like a lot of men (most men, I suspect) I had a wandering eye. After a couple of drinks at a golf club party I'd often get romantic ideas about some of the other women at the party, usually wives of my friends. I'm the kind of person who gets amorous under the influence of alcohol. I have friends who tend to get depressed or belligerent when they've had a few drinks; that never happens to me.

Sometimes, when in this amorous mood, I'd dance with a

woman, other than my wife, who was feeling similarly amorous. Whether these encounters ever led to anything more
is a subject on which I do not intend to comment, but one
thing is certain—they could never have led to the dissolution
of our marriage. By the time we had moved to Litchfield we
already had five children, and we'd gone through five difficult
years at Bellevue together. That held us together more firmly
than the most elaborate marriage vows could ever have done.
There were times when Joan got furious with me, and occasions when I wasn't especially happy with Joan, but after
just seven years it would have taken dynamite to dissolve
our marriage. (One of Joan's definitions of "dynamite" has
always been any *definite* evidence that I was involved with
another woman.)

If we were held together by shared experiences in our thirties, by the time I reached fifty and was in the midst of my
crisis our many more shared experiences had tied us together
so tightly that even "dynamite" (by Joan's definition) probably wouldn't have parted us. In raising six children through
their teens, you work together to solve so many crises that
you become a team—so much so that neither can function
well alone. In particular, having Joan with me as I went
through the trauma of discovering I had heart disease, followed by the bypass operation, seemed to almost mold us
into one being.

Most men in crisis, if they've been married ten years or
more, have the same sort of ties to their wives. However, in
the heat of sexual passion, in the depths of their depression,
some of them seem to forget these shared experiences. It's
as though they become blind to everything except the attractive qualities of the new woman. It's foolish, but it happens—partly, I think, because in our society such emphasis
is placed on sex, youth, and having a good time.

Every ad we see on television or in magazines suggests
that the major goal of all our lives is to stay dry, smell nice,

look attractive, be sexually alluring, and—above all—to have fun. "Fun" seems to be fancy dinners, swinging aprés-ski parties, ocean voyages, or racing along a country road in a big new car. That's about as much like real life as Peter Sellers's Inspector Clouseau is like a real-life policeman.

Real life is made up of week after week and year after year of work, play, coping with minor and major crises and, of course, lovemaking. In real life lovemaking takes up, at the most, 5/112 of the average week, for even the most sexually active couple. (That's 5 hours out of the 112 waking hours in a week; I've allowed 56 hours for sleeping.) The other things fill in the remaining 107/112. Isn't it crazy to make a major life change that is largely dependent on what goes on for 5 out of 112 waking hours each week?

I suppose, if we think about it at all, when most of us got married we expected that the erotic element in our relationship would last indefinitely, and it should. But not, for heaven's sake, at the same intensity as on our wedding night. If it did, we'd be all burned out in two or three years. That erotic intensity quite naturally diminishes over the years, though it should never disappear. As it dwindles, it's replaced by the companionship, the friendship, the shared memories, and the mutual interests that husband and wife develop. These are things that grow in intensity as we grow older. They're more than an adequate replacement for the eroticism. But they aren't glorified in the ads on television or the magazines; except as exemplified by the "reach out and touch someone" telephone ads that concentrate on a two-year-old saying "Goo-goo" to grandma and grandpa—characters with whom those of us in middle age certainly don't want to identify.

The pleasures of middle age (a life period that is lasting longer every year) are widely neglected by our society. The man in crisis is being foolish when he tries to reach back and reclaim the pleasures of his youth. He will almost certainly be better off if he clings to the less exciting but equally

satisfying joys of middle age; and, in most instances, with
the wife partner who has gone through the turbulent younger
years with him. Only she has shared, and can fully understand, the trials and tribulations, the pleasure and the pain,
the disappointments and the triumphs, that have been a large
part of all those years.

On the other hand, let's concede that a new woman may,
indeed, bring at least a temporary return of potency. After
ten, twenty, or thirty years of marriage only a dunce would
expect sex with the same woman to be as exciting as it once
was. You know each other too well. There's a lot to be said,
sexually, for knowing your partner well; you each know, or
ought to know, the other's sexual preferences. You don't waste
a lot of time doing things in bed that neither of you enjoy.

But, certainly, some of the initial excitement is gone. That
can't be helped. You're used to seeing your wife (or husband;
but remember this is the male crisis I'm writing about) naked;
that sight probably doesn't give you an instant erection. But
the bare breast of the attractive young woman from the secretarial pool may make you harder than you've been in a
long time. Lust is what that's called, not to be confused with
love. Are a couple of hours in a motel with a casual friend
to whom you're physically attracted apt to be disastrous for
your marriage?

That depends on several factors: (1) Are you going to feel
guilty about it? If so, will the guilt outweigh the pleasure?
(2) Can you keep it discreet, so that no one finds out? You
can't answer that with any certainty, of course, but is it at
least reasonably possible? (3) If your wife does find out, how
is it going to affect your marriage? Is she the sort of person
who will toss you out if she learns of one breach of fidelity?
Is she the kind who says, "Men will be men," and will put
up with it as long as you're not flagrant? Or does she fall
somewhere in the middle?

One of the things that amazed me, when I started hearing

from women with husbands in mid-life crisis, was how tolerant women were of their husbands' affairs. I can't remember a woman who wasn't willing to forgive a single transgression. Only two out of a hundred seemed willing to live with a husband who maintained a steady sexual relationship with another woman, but most women weren't concerned about casual one-night stands.

There is a poem, author unknown, that goes,

> Hogamous, higamous,
> Men are polygamous,
> Higamous, hogamous
> Women monogamous.

In 1984 it may sound chauvinistic to say that the poem may be accurate, but it is certainly true that women seem to accept at least the first two lines of the poem.

At first I thought these women were silly, that even an occasional casual affair would eventually lead to a situation that would destroy a marriage. Now, after talking to a lot of men, wives, and marriage counselors, I've changed my mind. My guess is that by fifty close to 100 percent of men have had at least one casual fling, even if it was only a one-night stand, and the evidence is that most marriages have survived it. In fact there's evidence that an outside affair is, in some instances, good for the sexual side of a man's marriage. The sexual rejuvenation he finds with the new woman persists in the sex life he and his wife enjoy. At one time, on a television show, Dr. Joyce Brothers said the same thing—that wives were sometimes the beneficiaries, sexually, of their husbands' outside affairs. Dr. Brothers was severely criticized for saying it (as I may be) but, after talking to a lot of men in mid-life crisis, I'm convinced that it's true.

What of the woman who is involved in this affair? Perhaps she went into it for the same reason he did—sexual attraction—and perhaps, like him, she too has fallen in love, or thinks she has. In many ways, she is the one who stands to lose the most in this affair.

Looked at from the point of view of the wife of the man in crisis, the younger woman, no matter what her intentions, is hunting on posted territory. Certainly, until very recently, a married man was considered (by other women, if not by the man himself) to be off limits to an unmarried woman. The single woman who got involved in an affair with a married man was looked upon as a homewrecker. She lost the respect of most other women. Marriage was still considered a sacred state, not one to be treated lightly.

Though the image of marriage has lost some of its sacred status in the 1980s, it is still generally true that women of all generations tend to look askance at the women who interfere in a marriage. Even in that bastion of avant-garde culture, *The New York Review of Books*, where there are regularly pages of ads by both gay and heterosexual men and women looking for suitable partners, the warning "No married men need apply" is often included. (Men, incidentally, in the ads they run, are likely not to exclude married women. In fact, many of the ads seem to be by married men looking for "a little something on the side," married or single. As Joan has said to me more than once, "Men are bastards.") So, even though the sanctity of marriage—particularly the monogamy that was once considered a critical element—is now under attack, the tradition is still strong enough to make it certain that the woman who threatens the stability of a marriage will be looked upon as an unwelcome, immoral transgressor. And most wives of men in crisis will agree that she should be.

Even granting all this, it is still true that sexual affairs outside the home, carried on discreetly when both parties are interested only in sex, may indeed be good for a man's potency and his sex life with his wife. On the other hand, such affairs are always unpredictable as to the course they'll take; no relationship stands still and if the man (or the woman) falls in love and wants the new partner all to himself, then this comfortable little affair can blow up into a moral, legal, and social disaster. Using an affair to restore one's potency is like using a stick of dynamite (excuse the analogy) to open a door. The door will certainly open, but it will probably be in splinters, as will the rest of the house.

Generally speaking, and knowing that in the 1980s they don't seem to be considered the moral and social catastrophes they once were, casual affairs are not recommended as treatment for men in crisis with potency problems. You run the risk of restoring the potency but destroying the marriage.

Here, for example, is what happened to one friend of mine who got "involved" during his mid-life crisis.

Abe was only thirty-five when he went into a slump. "Rose and I had been married ten years," he said, "and we had two kids: Tim, eight, and Marie, six. Great kids.

"We had gotten married when I was twenty-five, during my first year as an anesthesiology resident. I was reasonably paid—$20,000 a year—but I was $50,000 in debt from medical school, so there wasn't much left for the lush life. When I got into practice seven years ago, my income tripled.

"The hell of it was, my life also got boring. Everyone thinks medical practice is constantly exciting, but let me assure you it isn't. At the hospital where I work, we don't do cardiac surgery or neurosurgery. It's D. and C.'s, appendectomies, and hysterectomies. Do you know how anesthesiologists describe anesthesia practice? 'Two minutes of terror followed by two hours of boredom, followed by one minute of terror.' The only excitement comes when you put them to sleep and wake them up. After ten years, even those moments weren't very exciting. The thought of thirty more years of anesthesia seemed unbearable to me.

"But what could I do? To switch to another specialty would

have required anywhere from three to seven more years of residency, and neither Rose nor I were eager to go back to the tiny apartment, the every-other-night call schedule and chili three evenings a week. I couldn't see a way out. I'd lie awake nights, dreading the next day. The money was good— I was up to $90,000 a year, but I wondered how long I could take it.

"Rose and I started to quarrel. She couldn't understand why I was restless. 'You spent all those years training to be a doctor. You're good at what you do. Why can't you be satisfied?' I tried to explain, but she couldn't understand. She'd get angry when I mentioned the possibility of starting over. 'You're thirty-five,' she said, 'you'd be over forty before you got through another residency. We aren't going to live forever.'

"It got so we were arguing almost every night. We'd always had a great sex life, but now I found I just wasn't interested. My libido went to hell. A few times, after we'd both had a couple of drinks, we'd go to bed and I'd try to make love to her, but she wasn't always interested. Worse, when she was, I couldn't get it up. You can imagine how that made me feel.

"Then one evening, after I'd just finished a long hysterectomy case, I was cleaning up my equipment when Margo, who had been the scrub nurse on the case, came into the O.R. looking for some records. We'd worked together often and a few times I'd taken her out for a beer. She's an attractive woman, twenty-eight, long black hair, great figure, never been married. Had some opportunities, she told me, but Mr. Right hadn't come along yet. I guess she could tell I was down at the mouth because, for the first time, she asked me if I had time for a beer.

"No sense prolonging this. I said yes, told her my troubles and she gave me sympathy—just what I wanted. After three beers we went up to her apartment and I was so far from being impotent it was amazing. I had my beeper—I was on call that night—so I phoned Rose and told her there was an emergency coming in and I'd be spending the night at the hospital. I've never in my life had as much sex as I had in the next eight hours.

"When I told Margo how I felt about anesthesia, she agreed with me. 'I'm not a doctor,' she said, 'and I probably shouldn't say this, but it never seemed like much fun to me. Surgeons seem to have all the enjoyment and all the glamour.' When I told her I was thinking of shifting specialties she said, 'Why not? After all, you'd only be forty when you'd be ready to go back to practice. That's young.'

"That was exactly what I wanted to hear, of course, and we started an affair that night. For the next six months I was like a dog in heat. I literally saturated myself in sex. Rose caught on, of course, and in another six months we were divorced—not without a lot of bitter fighting, I'm afraid. She called Margo a 'scheming slut,' which made me absolutely furious.

"Now comes the sad part. Right after Rose divorced me, I married Margo, and two months after we were married, Margo was pregnant. I wanted her to get an abortion, but she wouldn't hear of it. She wanted a family, and she wanted it now. When I said something about changing specialties, she said, 'I guess that will have to wait, won't it? You can hardly afford to go back to a resident's pay with alimony and child support to pay.' And damn it, she was right.

"You want to know something else, Bill? Just between you and me, I'm not sure but what Rose wasn't right, too. In my heart of hearts, I've begun to wonder if Margo isn't a schemer. When I went to bed with her that first time, I sure as hell never thought I'd find myself locked up in a worse bind than I was before. I guess that's what happens when you forget that your brains are in your head and not between your legs."

It may have been true that Abe and Rose would and should have gotten a divorce—sometime. But certainly Abe, in the midst of a mid-life crisis that involved not only severe job dissatisfaction but an impotency problem, should never have made the critical decision to end his marriage when he did. Now he is in a situation from which only a miracle will extricate him.

A friend of mine who had recently come through a very trying mid-life crisis once said to me, "Bill, I think there ought to be a law declaring every man in mid-life crisis *non compis mentis*. He ought not to be allowed to make any major decisions until a panel of experts pronounces him well. A law like that would certainly prevent a lot of misery."

I agree.

JOB DISSATISFACTION

Job dissatisfaction is another of the disturbing elements of the male mid-life crisis.

Think about it. Most men spend at least eight hours a day five days a week at their jobs. Many men devote even more time to their work. The men with the most challenging jobs almost invariably work at them for longer hours than do those with mundane jobs. Ten-hour days are not at all unusual for doctors, lawyers, and business executives. In fact, generally speaking, the higher up the executive ladder the businessman is, the fatter the briefcase he takes home with him in the evening. By the time he is forty-five, and a prime candidate for a mid-life crisis, he has probably been working at his present job, or a related one, for about twenty years.

The chances are also excellent that he's sick of it. Let's assume that he is not a high-powered businessman, but a factory worker on an assembly line. Can you imagine how bored he must be with the repetitive drudgery he goes through every day? Imagine what it must be like tightening an endless stream of bolts, hour after hour, day after day, with only coffee breaks, weekends, and holidays to look forward to. I confess, I couldn't face it. Five years of that sort of thing would be enough to put me in an asylum.

So let's forget the assembly line and instead assume you're a lawyer with a small-town practice, like a friend of mine whom I'll call Al. One day Al is drawing up a will, the next he's defending someone who was caught while driving under the influence, the next he's helping a client get through a divorce. "Sounds like fun, doesn't it," Al said to me, "and for a while it is. But after twenty years, the thrill is gone. The first divorce is a challenge; the fiftieth is a bore. You've heard all the arguments, you can predict what the complaints are going to be, you've been down that road once too often.

"The hell of it is, you have to get yourself up for every case, because it's new and important to the client. That's difficult to do. For the first few years every case is exhilarating. After ten years, every case is exhausting. And in a small-town practice I'm never going to get the big, challenging cases—complex tax cases, for example—because people with complicated tax problems involving lots of money are going to go to one of the big firms with specialists who spend all their time practicing tax law. I should never have settled in a small town; but now I'm forty-five and it's too late to move. Bright young lawyers by the thousands are passing the bar. They're the ones the big firms will hire."

After I talked to Al, I talked to Max, who is a lawyer with a fifty-member firm and actually specializes in tax law. He's forty-five, too. "You can't believe how sick I am of tax law, Bill," he said. "I spend all day and part of most evenings looking for tax dodges to help our corporate clients save a few thousand dollars. The way the tax laws have been changing I have to spend most weekends just keeping up with what's happening. Every day it's the same thing. Sure, I'm an expert, but an expert at only one small part of the law. I can tell you this: if I had it to do again, I'd never join a big

firm. I'd open up an office in some small town were I could
get to know the people. One day I'd draw up a will, the next
I might defend some client who got caught for drunken driving, the next I'd be handling a divorce. Maybe once in a while
I'd help some guy figure out his tax form, but I wouldn't be
doing it every day. Twenty years of the same damn problem
day after day after day is more than anyone should have to
stand."

So it goes; everyone thinks the other person's job is more
interesting, more challenging, more gratifying than his. The
fact is that after twenty years any job becomes a bit wearing.

In my case I have to admit that, if I hadn't started writing
for publication, I think I would have left Litchfield back in
1970, after ten years of practice. Sure, I have a surgical practice that is very broad. One day I may put in a hip prosthesis
and do a hemorrhoidectomy. The next I perform a hysterectomy. The next, I take out a thyroid tumor. I have a lot of
variety in my practice.

But after ten years a lot of the thrill is gone. The first
appendectomy is extremely challenging. The fiftieth is con-
siderably less so. And in a small hospital you can hardly be
on the cutting edge (so to speak) of surgery. I'm never going
to do a coronary artery bypass; I'm not going to transplant
a kidney; I'm not going to put in an artificial knee. I'm going
to continue to do gall bladders, appendectomies, and hernias.
Each case will be a little bit different from the preceding
one, and every patient will be grateful for what I've done;
those are the things that make surgery perhaps the least
boring of all jobs. Still, after ten years, most of the time you're
going to be repeating yourself. After twenty, you're bound to
be bored.

About ten years ago, when I was in a restless mood, I
decided I'd like to move back to New England. Joan said, "If
that's what you want, it's all right with me." That night I
wrote an advertisement that went something like this:

44-year-old board-certified general surgeon seeks to relo-
cate in New England, preferably within 75 miles of Boston. I
have 12 years of experience as the only surgeon in Litchfield,
a rural Minnesota city. For details, call or write ...

I listed my phone number and address.

A day or two after the ad appeared in the *New England
Journal of Medicine*, I had many letters and phone calls from
all over the United States, including big metropolitan areas
and small to moderate-size cities in both New England and
California. Unfortunately (or fortunately; who's to say?) none
of the writers or callers were offering me a position in New
England. Without exception each respondent wanted to know
how soon I'd be leaving Litchfeld, because they wanted to
take my place.

I can assure you that this response prompted me to re-
consider my situation. After listing the pros and cons I decided Litchfield was a pretty nice place after all.

But the man in mid-life crisis almost invariably feels trapped in his job. Take Al, for example. He is absolutely correct
when he says that it would be difficult to give up his small-
town practice and find a position as a tax attorney for a big
firm. Just as it would be difficult for Max to move to a small
town and build a general practice. It would have been equally
difficult for me to leave Litchfield, move to a big city, and
enter the academic world of surgery. For any man in mid-
life, a radical change of careers is always difficult. Not only
because it takes time to learn how to do the new work and
to find a position, but because any such shift is almost certainly going to require at least a temporary reduction in
income, just when financial demands are at their peak.

For example, if the man of forty-five has children they are
likely to be of college age. Board, room, and tuition—if he
wants to provide those things for his children—are going to
require a substantial portion of his income. If he makes a

career move that requires a salary reduction, either the children's education is going to go unfinanced, or he's going to have to cut back on his life-style in some other way.

That's difficult to do. Much as Al might want to move to a big city and become a tax expert, it's unlikely that he'll want to give up his nice home for a tiny apartment, trade his Cadillac in for a Volkswagen, and give up his country club membership. Career shifts in mid-life are usually an either-or proposition; either you stick with your job and your pleasant life-style, or you shift careers and lower your life-style. Only those who are independently wealthy can have it both ways.

Let's think about them for a moment—those lucky men who don't have to worry about money, who have so much of it that they would have to work day and night to spend it all. The money doesn't protect them from mid-life crises— most of us can think of dozens of wealthy men who have been through such crises—but money is not something that they have to dwell on. If a man has 10 million dollars and he has to give his wife 5 million dollars in order to get divorced and marry his new young girl friend, so be it. He'll be able to live comfortably on the remaining 5 million. (I suspect that having a great deal of money actually allows some men to make foolish crisis decisions they wouldn't have made otherwise. The man with a net worth of $40,000 and a salary of $25,000 is going to think long and hard about breaking up his home, if only because he knows it will be next to impossible to support two households on his income. The fact that he can't afford it may be the one thing that prevents him from making a foolish decision he'll later regret.)

For most men in crisis, money is a major concern. Not, in most cases, because he hasn't enough money to leave his wife, but because he can't see any way he's ever going to be able to afford the things he once thought he'd have for his wife, his children, and himself. Let's assume that at fifty, with a wife and three children, he's earning $50,000 a year; well above average for a fifty-year-old man these days, but hardly enough to allow him to buy a Mercedes or even the home with the tennis court and swimming pool he always expected to have. He has a middle-level management job and his best guess is that that is where he's going to spend the rest of his career. He'll continue to get annual raises and/ or bonuses, but just enough to keep him in the comfortable but not wealthy situation in which he currently lives. At fifty, with another twenty-five years of life ahead, that may seem like a pretty glum prognosis. What can you say to such a man?

One thing that is not worth saying is, "Think of how much better off you are than those poor people in Calcutta"—or Appalachia, or Zimbabwe, or anywhere else. That will be absolutely no consolation to any man. He's a lot less well off, financially, than Johnny Carson or Frank Sinatra and he's going to stay that way. He never expected to be as poor as the people in Calcutta; he did hope to be a lot wealthier than he is. That's why he's disappointed.

"At least you've got your health," is another cliché that's definitely no help to the man in crisis. A man who enjoys good health takes it for granted. It doesn't seem to him like something for which he should be particularly grateful. The fact that he's physically able to swim will not make him feel better about not having his own private pool to swim in.

The one helpful thing I've found to ask men in crisis who are brooding over their relative (to Carson, et al.) poverty is this: "Over the last fifty years have you ever found any cor- relation between your income and your happiness?" Once in a while someone says "Yes"—usually someone who not only had a particularly poverty-stricken childhood, but had par- ents who were mean. When pressed, even these people will admit that it was their parents' meanness and not the poverty that made them unhappy. Many kids who grow up in poor families have a lot of fun. Outsiders might think they should be miserable, but they aren't.

At least 95 percent of the people I've asked, many of whom were men in crisis, will admit that their happiness has never been directly proportional to their income. When they were relatively poor, they were sure they'd be happier when they had more money, but when they had more money they were neither more nor less happy than they had been. Naturally, they then thought they didn't have quite enough money to bring them happiness, but—surprise!—when they had quite a bit more, they still weren't any more happy. At least, not because of the money. Once they'd had the new Mercedes for a couple of months, they had to admit it wasn't that much more comfortable than the old Chevy. As soon as they had the big, fancy house, they realized that, since you lived in only one room at a time, it didn't really give them any more pleasure than their bungalow had. When they had the private pool, they found the water wasn't any more refreshing than it had been at the public pool. What's more, the kids didn't even want to swim in the backyard pool; they preferred to go uptown to the public pool, so they could be with their friends.

Personally, I'd have a tough time saying which period in my life was the happiest. Joan and I had a wonderful time when I was an intern, earned $65 a month, and lived in the $65-a-month railroad flat at 526 E. 82nd Street, with cockroaches running out of the refrigerator. On hot afternoons Joan used to visit air-conditioned hotels in downtown Manhattan and sit in the lobby and people watch. Chili three nights a week was fine with me. I like chili.

When we lived in Igloo, South Dakota, and I was a captain in the army medical corps, we had a wonderful time. We had our own little army house and the kids could run all over the open fields. We had great times with the other people in Igloo.

When we went back to New York after two years, my income dropped from whatever it was they paid an army captain in 1957, to $125 a month, which was what a surgical resident at Bellevue was paid. We lived out in Eastchester in a two-bedroom rent-controlled apartment into which Joan and I and the five kids were squeezed, but we had a marvelous time. Instead of drinking Vat 69, which we had drunk in Igloo, I switched to Mill Road Scotch, named after the store where they sold it (heaven only knows where it came from), but that didn't make us any less happy. I look back on those days in Eastchester with great nostalgia, as does Joan.

When we moved to Litchfield in 1960, my starting salary as the board surgeon for the Litchfield Clinic was $12,000, about four times what I had made in Bellevue in 1959. You know what? That money went just as fast as the $3,000 I'd made the previous year. Was I any happier? No. Just as happy as I'd been, I guess, but not happier. I had loved Bellevue.

That's the way it's gone over the last twenty-three years. Both as a writer and a surgeon, my income has fluctuated rather markedly. Sometimes I have quite a good year, sometimes not so good—financially speaking, of course. But if you asked me to plot my happy years and less than happy years, and see how they matched my salary, I can guarantee there'd be no correlation. As I remember it, the time of my mid-life crisis, one of my few miserable years, came at a time when my income was unusually high. I suspect that anyone who thinks income and happiness are directly correlated will be surprised to find that there is no such relationship.

If you can get the man in crisis to think about that, it may cheer him up a bit. He may still be disappointed that he isn't going to become president of the company, but it won't be because he thinks the increased salary would have made him happy. *That* will mean one less illusion to live with.

At least Al and Max and I considered career shifts that were realistic. None of us even contemplated the kind of drastic change that he might have preferred if he had been less sensible.

For example, Tom, at fifty, decided he couldn't face one more day as a car dealer. He had always been a movie buff so he sold his car agency and bought a movie theater. He hadn't the faintest notion of how the movie business worked, but he lucked out. The theater he bought was an art theater, in an excellent location, and he managed to find an experienced manager to join him in the venture. His income was reduced, and so was his life-style, but he survived. As it turned out he and his wife, Mary, seem to be happier now than they have been in years.

When I talked to Tom recently he said, "I've never regretted the move. My two daughters and my son had to go to the University of Minnesota instead of Macalester, where they'd planned to go, but it turned out that they liked the university very much. They also told us—each kid independently—that they were so happy to see their mother and me getting along better that attending a different college was a small price for them to pay. That convinced Mary and me that we'd done the right thing.

"To be perfectly honest, the movie business isn't as fascinating as I hoped it would be. There's a lot of paper work and drudgery to it, but I enjoy meeting with distributors and other theater owners, and I like the hours. I'm home with my family a lot more than I once was. I can tell you this: running a movie theater is, for me, a lot more fun than selling cars was."

If the job change you're thinking of making is one that you hope will produce more income, but will require more time and/or traveling from you, think about it carefully. Perhaps your kids are about to leave home for college and your wife is thinking of launching a career of her own; if so, all well and good. But if your kids are still at home and your wife is tied up with their activities, a job that will keep you away from them most of the time may well prove to be a very bad idea. We pass this way only once, your kids are in grade and high school only once, and when those years end you'll be surprised at how infrequently you'll see them.

It's sad to discover how many men think, mistakenly, that they are doing all they should for their wives and children by supplying them with cars, a nice home, a prep school education, and plenty of spending money. When you see these families at crisis centers, either because one of the parents has become an alcoholic or one of the kids has gotten hooked on drugs, almost invariably the father is shocked to find that his wife and kids feel as if he neglected them. "We never got to know you, Dad," one nineteen-year-old boy, in for drug addiction, told his father. "You were always gone when Jimmy and Danny and I were growing up." His father was heart-broken. He'd have been a lot better off if he'd passed up the promotion that took him away from his family so much of the time. Sure, kids like fancy cars and clothes, but give them a choice between those things and a close relationship with their father and they'll take the latter every time.

There's no question that it's possible to take the promo-tion, make the move, provide well for the kids, and still be close to them. Possible, but often very, very difficult. Think about those difficulties before you jump at that new, chal-lenging job.

For some reason the idea of opening a restaurant tempts a lot of men at mid-life crisis time. There doesn't seem to be a man or woman alive who doesn't think he or she is capable of becoming a successful restauranteur. "I tell you what I'd like to do," my friend Keith said to me, "I'd like to buy that bank just off Main Street—the old Northwestern Bank. I could put the bar where the president's office was and put booths where the teller cages used to be. There's plenty of room in the back for the kitchen.

"I'd stick to steak, chicken and, for lunch, soup and sandwiches. Big, thick, sandwiches, not like the ones you get at the Cozy Cat Café. And the drinks would be big, too, served in those nice heavy glasses. Of course we'd serve popovers at dinner. I love popovers." (People who think of starting restaurants always have some specialty, such as popovers, that they think will make their restaurant a success.)

Keith, an airline pilot, has, of course, absolutely no understanding of how the restaurant business works. When he thinks of it he thinks, as most of us do, of standing at the door greeting a steady stream of customers every evening and then, later, returning to his office to count the money and put the profits in the safe. He doesn't think of the difficulties of finding and paying trained and reliable help, of buying the fresh meats and vegetables, of creating menus that will ensure the return of his customers, of arranging for dishwashers and garbage disposal.

Nevertheless, job dissatisfaction is a major part of most male mid-life crises, and it must be dealt with wisely and sympathetically.

In some societies, as men and women grow older they assume an increasingly exalted role. Because of their experience and wisdom younger members turn to them for advice and counsel. In our society this occasionally happens—it's usually the older men who are the chief executive officers and senior vice presidents of major corporations—but these men are the exception. They represent far less than 1 percent of the work force. The other 99 percent, men of fifty or sixty—even forty—who have not made it to the top are looked upon with disdain (or think they are, which can be equally devastating). We have a rat-race society and only the winners get the rewards, emotional or financial, for which everyone in our culture is trained to strive.

It's sad, and it's one of the major reasons why the male mid-life crisis is such a prevalent condition. I have a friend— I'll call him Phil—who exemplifies exactly what I mean.

Phil went to work for an insurance company—I'll call it Monarch Insurance Company—at twenty-five. After college he had first tried his hand at journalism, but decided reluctantly that he wasn't much of a writer and, since he was an outgoing, reasonably aggressive person, he thought he might do well in insurance.

He started working as an agent in a small town and he did do well. After two years the company moved him to a bigger city and, after another five years, he had his own agency in a town of 15,000. At thirty-two, he was married and had three children. He was earning a good living and his superiors in the company seemed to like him. At thirty-seven they offered him a job as a district manager. This meant moving to a city of 100,000, and it meant more time on the road. His income wouldn't go up much; in fact, since he had a flourishing agency in the small town, it would at least temporarily mean a small cut in pay. Phil and Pat, his wife, were reluctant to leave their small town, but Phil said, "Look, if I don't make this move I may not get another chance. Eventually I'd like to get to a senior vice presidency and to do that I have to stay on track." Reluctantly, Pat agreed to the move.

Five years later, at forty-two, Phil was offered the job of regional manager. Pat and his three children didn't want to make the move—this time to a city of 500,000—but again, Phil said, "If I say no, I'm here forever. I want to move up." So they went.

Four years later a vice president's job became available

and Phil expected to get it. After two months of rumors and intra-office competition, the president of the company moved another regional manager into the job. Phil could have tolerated this except for one thing: the man to whom the job was given was thirty-eight, eight years younger than Phil. All Phil could do was go on with his work, hoping and praying that the next vice presidency would be his. Two years later, when Phil was forty-eight, a job as vice president did become available and this time Phil wasn't even seriously considered. A forty-two-year-old regional manager was moved in from another part of the country.

It then became apparent to Phil that, despite twenty-three years of devotion to Monarch Insurance, he had gone as far up the ladder as he was going to go. He would be a regional manager until he was fifty-nine, at which age he could retire. He could either accept that fact and go on with his work, or quit and try doing something else. But he was forty-eight— too late, he felt, to start another career. He was trapped, or so he felt. Phil then began a mid-life crisis of titanic proportions. Before it ended Phil, Pat, and their three children went through hell.

A similar fate befell Joe, an accountant with a California based company I'll call Alvams, a large construction firm that does work all over the country. Some of their projects— building dams, constructing freeways, erecting bridges—take three or four years to complete. At the age of forty-five, after twenty years with the firm, Joe and his family had lived in six different cities in various parts of the United States. It had been a nomadic life, but Joe didn't mind it and his family went along with it.

By then Joe was a vice president and he thought he had a reasonable chance to become president in another five years, when the current president planned to retire. At that time— 1976—his company decided to go international. Joe was in charge of preparing a bid to do road construction in Nigeria, a project that would probably last three years. Joe was asked if he would move to Nigeria as the on-site head man for the duration of the project. He agreed.

Nigeria, much as the natives may like it, is not a country in which the life-style appeals to most Westerners. Joe tolerated it because most of every day and evening was devoted to his work. His wife, Temple, hated every minute she spent in the country. As construction jobs often do, this one lasted longer than was anticipated. Joe and Temple didn't get back to the United States to stay until the middle of 1981, almost five years after they left.

In the meantime, things at Alvams had moved along other tracks. When Joe came back everyone congratulated him on the fine job he'd done, but he also found that the politics of business had shifted so that a forty-five-year-old engineer was now in line for the president's job. Joe would get a raise and a position of responsibility, but it was clear he was never going to be president. Joe took that blow hard. He had wanted to be president, not so much for the money but for the prestige and for the chance to prove to himself and others that he was capable of running the entire operation. When it didn't happen, he went into a mid-life crisis that lasted almost two years.

I suppose it's only natural for the employee to blame the company when things like this happen, but looked at objectively the company is not at fault. After all, there may be ten or twenty vice presidents from which one president is to be chosen, and all twenty vice presidents may be men or women who could do the job satisfactorily. It is probably impossible to predict which of the twenty will make the best president. The decision can't be anything but an educated guess.

The point of all this is simply to emphasize that in the United States we take far too seriously the idea that we must "make it"—in business, the intellectual life, in social circles. It would be different if we could so control our lives that every step we took would lead inexorably to the next step and we would climb to whatever pinnacle we hoped to reach. That's not so. There are too few pinnacles, too many people who want to reach them, and too many factors beyond our control that can interfere with the progress we've planned.

It's silly for the man who has been passed by for a promotion to take it personally, but it's also understandable. When it happens, as it does to most of us, he'll need a lot of reassurance from his friends and family to convince him that someone else's success does not mean that he has been a failure. Is it any wonder that in our prestige-mad society, the male mid-life crisis is a raging epidemic?

The first thing that a man dissatisfied with his job ought to do is to write down the good things about it: his income; his vacation time; the retirement program; the chances of advancement. Some of these things certainly must be attractive or he wouldn't have stuck at it for ten or fifteen years.

Now write down the negative things. Boredom will probably lead the list. Next may come "little chance for advancement." Salary may also be discouraging; it's certainly not as great as you envisioned when you first went to work. Perhaps the retirement program, though appealing, is so far off that you can't bear the idea of waiting for it.

Next, list your qualifications for other jobs: your experience; your record of reliability; perhaps some skills that you haven't used in your current job—the ability to speak a second language, for example, or perhaps an innate ability as a mechanic that your job hasn't called for.

Now list the possible career shifts you might make, both those in which your income would stay the same and those in which your income would probably be less, simply because of the nature of the job. The latter doesn't necessarily preclude a career shift. I know, for example, one lawyer in his mid-forties, with a very successful law firm, who decided to quit and become a reporter for a small-town newspaper at half the salary. The pleasure he got from his career shift more than compensated for the reduced income.

List the career shifts in which, initially, your income would decline, but eventually might be expected to increase. An engineer friend of mine who had been successful dabbling in the stock market made that kind of shift. He took a 70 percent cut in his engineer's salary to become a stockbroker, but two years after he became a broker he was earning twice what he had as an engineer.

Consider whether you're ready to move—to leave your friends and relatives behind, uproot your children, take your wife away from her friends and, if she's working, her job. Twice over the last twenty years, Joan and I considered moving (I had received very appealing offers to join surgical groups in other states) and both times the deciding factors in persuading us to stay in Litchfield were our kids. All six were involved in extracurricular activities, loved Litchfield, had lots of friends, and we didn't think it was fair to drag them away. You can get advice both ways: some people will swear that moving in the middle of high school didn't bother their kids at all; others will say just as positively that their lives were in turmoil for a year or more. Based on what I've read and people I've talked to, a lot depends on the children. If they're deeply involved in school activities, uprooting them can make what might otherwise have been a very pleasant year into one that is absolutely miserable.

One evening, as I sat at the golf club having a beer with Stan Roeser, the editor of our local newspaper and one of my closest friends, we got on the subject of moving: how it would offer a new challenge, how it would affect our children, what financial sacrifices it might entail. Then Stan made a good point. "One of the things I don't like about the idea of moving," he said, "is that it takes about five years in a new town to figure out who's really full of bullshit."

I laughed, but I had to agree with him. Both Stan and I

had been in Litchfield long enough to know how much credence to give to the various people we met and talked with. Just for the fun of it, we each took out a pen and listed the names of the people we considered the five biggest bullshitters in town, and when we exchanged lists we had four names in common. We even agreed that the two we had listed differently would have appeared on each other's list if we'd gone to six. Stan thought that the job of learning again who the bull artists were in a new town was a negative factor to consider, and I agreed. (Probably both Stan and I would show up with some frequency if other Litchfield residents made out similar lists, but that doesn't alter my point.)

Caution is particularly necessary if the male in mid-life crisis is in a depression, drinking heavily, or is distracted from his work by another woman. With those complicating factors, he may tend to misevaluate his job.

On the other hand, a career change may well be the answer to his mid-life crisis. With a new job—one that requires all his energy and skill—he may find that he neither needs nor wants the solace of the bottle or an extramarital affair. If the job requires a geographic shift, that too may be helpful in pulling a man through a mid-life crisis.

Let me repeat, this is not a decision to be made lightly. Giving up the known for the unknown is always difficult if it means leaving friends, neighbors, and relatives behind. No matter how carefully you prepare, you're likely to overlook something of importance. You may not realize until you have moved just how much that weekly Great Books discussion meant to your social life. Be prepared for some episodes of loneliness. They're inevitable.

When you've made all these lists, show them to your wife and, if it seems appropriate, to your children. Certainly your wife will have some considerations of her own to add to the lists, and possibly your children's reaction to what you've listed may surprise you. In any case, do the best you can to include all the effects a career change may cause.

Then spend at least two weeks thinking about what the change would mean and talking it over with your wife, children, and—possibly—close friends who may know more about these career options than you do. After two or three weeks of study, make your decision. If you decide not to make a career shift, fine. Forget about it and get on with your life. If you decide to make the move, get organized and do so. In either case promise yourself that, whatever happens, you're not going to let yourself be obsessed with second guesses. There is nothing less rewarding than worrying about whether or not you've made a mistake.

Having said all this, let me add that most counselors, and many highly respected men who are not in the counseling business, think that a career shift every ten years is probably the best possible way to live one's life. Admittedly, it's difficult to do; after ten or fifteen years a man is often just reaching that point in his career when he's recognized as an authority. It's difficult to give that up.

What seems to work best is to make a career shift that is not a complete break with what you've done. If you're a mechanic who has always worked for a big company, maybe now is the time to start your own shop; if you're an insurance salesman, perhaps it's time you considered becoming a stockbroker; if you're a tax lawyer, maybe you ought to try shifting into the criminal defense division; if you're a general surgeon, perhaps you ought to take a six-month fellowship in hand surgery and start concentrating on hand injuries. There are a lot of mild to moderate shifts into what Gail Sheehy calls "parallel" careers that most of us can make to rejuvenate interest in our work.

And if a parallel shift isn't what you want, then it may be that the radical change is right for you. As long as you and your wife fully understand what that shift may mean to your life-style, for heaven's sake, take the chance. At forty-five or even fifty-five, you don't have to stay stuck in a rut. With proper preparation (take a couple of courses in restaurant management, or work for a month or two at a movie theater, or talk with the owner of a bookstore) get rid of the insurance agency or the car dealership that is making you so miserable and buy the restaurant, the movie theater, or the bookstore. You probably won't live as high as you once did, but the chances are you'll have a lot more fun.

Assuming, of course, you stay healthy. Health—and fear of death—are major concerns of the male at mid-life.

MORTALITY

I have never met a man over forty who hasn't, at least once, wondered if he was having a heart attack. Chest pains are extremely common and most of them are of no significance, but men fear heart attacks just as much as women fear breast cancer. Any time a man over thirty-five has an unexplained attack of pain or even soreness in his chest, he will, at least fleetingly, wonder if it could possibly be the first sign of an imminent heart attack.

The man in crisis worries not only about heart attacks, but about all the other physical conditions that might cripple or even kill him. He's at the age at which he will probably start reading the obituary column regularly. Undoubtedly, one or two of his friends or acquaintances have died by now, and any time he sees the obituary of a man of about his age he'll think, "Gee, that could be me." If anyone is extremely mortality conscious, it's the man in crisis.

The hell of it is, he's right. When you get into your forties and fifties your body does begin to run down. There's no sense in pretending otherwise. All those books that claim that, with care, you can stay physically youthful well into your sixties are nonsense. If that were the case, Julius Boros, Arnold Palmer, and Sam Snead would still be playing in the open golf tournaments, instead of competing in the Senior Division. Rod Laver and Ken Rosewall would be at Wimbledon trying to knock off John McEnroe and Jimmy Connors, instead of playing in tournaments limited to those over forty. Frank Gifford would be scoring touchdowns instead of arguing with Howard Cosell. There is no fountain of youth, no elixir that will make a forty-five-year-old body as resilient, agile, and untiring as that of a twenty-five-year-old. It's silly to pretend that there is.

Which doesn't mean that the man in mid-life ought to sit around waiting for that heart attack to strike. It doesn't mean that it's wise to brood over the obituary column nor that he ought to just give up on life, as so many men in crisis are inclined to do. That would be even sillier than pretending he's going to be eternally youthful.

As we've already mentioned, the man in crisis who is worried about his health (and that means 99 percent of all men in crisis) should have a thorough physical examination. If there is something wrong with him—a touch of high blood pressure, early diabetes, maybe a little arthritis—he can get appropriate treatment that will remedy or alleviate the condition. In 1900 or even in 1930 there wasn't much that could be done to treat most diseases. We didn't have any pills that would lower blood pressure; diabetes treatment was just coming into its own; arthritis inevitably led to crippling. Now, if there's one thing the medical profession has, it's plenty of medicines and operations that can keep people alive and agile for many, many years. Only a fool would sit around and let death creep up on him when he could do so much to avoid it.

Once again, I'll use myself as an example. When I had that first attack of angina, in 1975, and appropriate studies showed that it was due to almost total blockage of two of the arteries to my heart, I didn't hesitate for a moment in deciding to have a bypass operation done. I'd studied the operation, it seemed like a reasonable operation to me, and even though it had then been in use for only seven years the early results were very promising. That operation gave me seven great, active years that wouldn't have been available to me just twenty years ago. I would have been a fool not to take advantage of that progress. No one can say with certainty that I would have been dead by 1980 if I hadn't had the operation, but the statistics certainly suggest that that would have been the case. (How long my second bypass operation—a quadruple—done in 1982 will add to my longevity, we'll have to wait and see.)

Harry Hopman, the famous tennis coach who led Australia to all those Davis Cup championships in the 1950s and 1960s, is still, at seventy-seven, running a tennis camp in Florida and is out on the courts hitting tennis balls every day. A few years ago his hips were so badly crippled by arthritis that he would have been confined to a wheelchair in a few months, if it had been 1964. Instead, he had both hips replaced and leads a happy, fulfilling, pain-free life.

Stories like Harry Hopman's are quite common today. Angry as we may get at the members of the medical profession because they charge too much, won't spend time with patients, don't seem to care about people (all accusations that are true of some doctors), one thing must be conceded: they can do a great deal for patients in 1984 that they couldn't do in 1924.

They cannot, however, stop the aging process. Maybe one day we'll have a pill that can accomplish that feat, but it's not currently available. In fact, doctors can't even slow down the aging process. Patients, however, can.

This is what the man in mid-life must realize. Instead of sitting around moping about impending death, he ought to do what he can to keep it at bay. This means regular exercise, a reasonable calorie intake, moderation in alcohol consumption and, preferably, no cigarettes. I'm not going to spend time in this book telling anyone how to exercise or how to eat. There are literally hundreds of books on these subjects available. None, as far as I know, will do you any harm, but none is necessary either. All you have to know about exercise is that it should be done regularly, preferably at least every other day, and it should be vigorous enough and last long enough to raise your heart rate to a moderate degree. As far as diet is concerned, just remember that your body needs a mixture of carbohydrates, fats, and proteins, and that calories do count. I don't care what else the diet does; if it supplies fewer calories in a day than you burn in a day, you'll lose weight. If calorie intake exceeds output, you'll gain weight. There's really nothing else you need to know because, if your diet is reasonably balanced, you'll get all the vitamins and minerals you'll need. The man in mid-life isn't going to improve his health or well-being one iota by gorging himself on vitamin and mineral supplements.

The man in mid-life whose father and/or uncles and/or grandfathers died at about his age is particularly likely to go into a slump, worrying about death. After all, he may have their genes.

His concern is understandable. However, he should ask himself what they died of. If it was an infectious disease, an accident, or pernicious anemia, then he doesn't have to worry about their deaths.

If the cause of their death was a condition that wasn't curable then, but is now, he shouldn't worry about it either. If it was a condition that doesn't run in families, i.e., there isn't any familial predisposition to the disease, he can forget that, too. Most cancers, for example, are not genetically linked.

Coronary artery heart disease, unfortunately, does seem

to run in families. My father died of it at fifty-eight and his brother at sixty-one. What keeps me from getting depressed about this is the fact that we now have medicines that we know will protect our hearts from the rhythm disturbances that are actually the cause of most "heart attack" deaths and, of course, the bypass operation. We also know that there are certain things we can do to prevent or at least slow down the development of coronary artery disease: control high blood pressure; keep weight at respectable levels; avoid cigarettes, for example—and I do those things. Maybe I won't live any longer than my father did, but I'll do what I can to try. Within limits—and that's something the man in mid-life ought to think about.

After all, there are only so many pleasures in life and you have to ask yourself, "Do I really want to give up this pleasure, or undertake this painful procedure, just to possibly add a year or two to my life?" Maybe not.

For example, if smoking cigarettes is one of the things you find most pleasurable in life, do you really want to give it up just so that you won't run quite so great a risk of developing lung cancer twenty years from now? After all, the vast majority (at least 99.8 percent) of cigarette smokers don't get lung cancer. So maybe the cigarettes taste so good to you that you're willing to run that extra little risk. That's your business. If you want to do it, enjoy the cigarette and stop worrying about lung cancer.

And your weight. Maybe you just love rich desserts. Okay, let's agree that if you satisfy your desire for rich desserts you're going to average ten pounds more than you would otherwise. Let's even agree that that raises the likelihood of your dying a year earlier than you would otherwise by 1 percent. (That, by the way, has never been proven.) So if you like desserts, then run that tiny risk. It's worth it to you.

I once spoke at a medical meeting at which Nathan Pritikin, the guru of Pritikin diet fame, was also a guest speaker.

Now I agree that Pritikin's regimen—diet and exercise, to put it succinctly—will keep a person relatively thin and fit. However, from what I've heard and read of his program, the only way to follow it faithfully is to make diet and exercise the most important considerations in your life. I just don't believe most people want to do that, or will do it for very long. I've talked to a lot of Pritikin enthusiasts just after they've started on his regimen; they can't say enough in praise of their new life-style. Almost invariably, in my experience, they're off the regimen and back to their old life-style within two years.

When Pritikin and I met at this meeting, we happened to sit at the same table at lunch. I'd already had my first bypass at that time, and I was eating and enjoying a luncheon of meat, potatoes, and vegetables with ice cream for dessert. All Pritikin ate was a bunch of grapes. He was a nice enough fellow, in my opinion, but not once during that meeting did I see him smile or laugh. If I have to eat grapes for lunch and become very solemn in order to live possibly an extra six months, I'll pass.

Let's assume you absolutely hate exercise, as I hate jogging. You know that if you exercise you may (*may*, I say, not *will*) live six months or a year longer than you will if you don't exercise. Is it worth all the misery of all that jogging just to live to be 75 instead of 74½? If it is, jog. If not, relax in your comfortable chair and read a book.

I heard a speaker once say that if you ran ten miles a day every day after you turned forty-five, you'd live an extra three years. The only catch is, you'd have spent four years of your life running. I don't know if those figures work out, or even if I remember them as he gave them, but the point of the story is plain—and I love it.

The male in mid-life, instead of dwelling on thoughts of death and disability, ought to concentrate on getting as much enjoyment out of every day as he can. Sure, at mid-life there aren't as many years to look forward to as there were, and you suddenly become conscious of that fact. All the more important to remember that old cliché: there's a lot more to life than living.

A man in mid-life ought to skip the obituary column and read the comics instead.

SEVEN

Advice for the Wife of the Man Whose Crisis Won't End

CONSIDERING THE BREAK

Now it's time to consider in depth the options of the woman who is married to a man in mid-life crisis. Let us assume, as is sometimes the case, that despite all the support the man receives from his wife, family, business associates, friends, and support groups, he continues the destructive behavior that is part of a mid-life crisis. One year goes by—then another six months—then another three months—and he is still neglecting his work, carrying on extramarital affairs, drinking excessively, behaving like an adolescent. His crisis has gone on so long that it is no longer reasonable to consider it a crisis; what has happened is that the man has undergone a complete personality change. Now his wife has to make a decision: does she stick with this man or does she cut her losses and get out?

I would estimate that perhaps 80 percent of men who go through a mid-life crisis revert to "normal" in a year or two, but the 20 percent who don't constitute a major problem. The flood of mail I received as a result of the articles published in *McCall's* and *Reader's Digest* came, with few exceptions, from women who were married to men whose mid-life crises showed no signs of ending. These women felt trapped. They didn't want to desert their husbands. On the other hand, their lives were rapidly becoming intolerable. What, they asked me, should they do?

There aren't any rigid rules as to how long a woman should stay with and support a man in crisis. In individual cases it will depend to a large extent on the personalities of both people. However, since there's a natural reluctance to make radical changes in one's life-style, some women keep throwing good years after bad, indefinitely. I think it's important to at least set a tentative schedule. Here is what I've recommended. (All recommendations are based on the hypothetical situation of a marriage that has lasted ten years and involves not only the man and the wife but two children. For shorter or longer marriages, fewer or more children, modifications might be appropriate.)

(1) If the marriage has never been a happy one, and is now very painful, give the man six months.

(2) If it has been a happy marriage, and is now very painful, give it a year.

(3) If it has been happy, and isn't too distressing even now, give it eighteen months.

(4) If it has been happy, is now bad, but is beginning to get a little better, give it two years.

(5) If it has been happy, is now not happy but is barely tolerable, and if you've already given it two years, then decide whether you're willing to live this way indefinitely. After two years it's unlikely that the relationship is going to change much—not, at least, for several more years.

Let me make it very clear that, generally speaking, I am not an advocate of divorce. I think in the eighties the attitude toward divorce is far too casual. When even minor disturbances occur in a marriage, as they inevitably do, one or both partners is likely to think, "Well, there's always divorce." Thirty or forty years ago divorce wasn't even considered an option in many families. Now it's likely to lead the list of options when a married couple aren't getting along as well as they would like.

I suppose, as I look back on our lives together, Joan and I went through some situations—weeks or even a few months in duration—which might, in the 1980s, have led many couples to consider divorce. I never considered it nor, she assures me, did she. Not because we weren't angry or upset enough, but simply because we'd grown up in an era and in families in which divorce was not considered an option. And even if we hadn't had that sort of background, I am sure that having six children would have made us think long and hard before divorcing. Admittedly, there are situations in which divorce of the parents is better for the children than growing up in a home in which the parents actively dislike each other. However, I think that divorce "for the sake of the children; to give them a more pleasant home environment" is often just so much nonsense. A husband and wife who stick together for the sake of their children, providing a united home, may be making a sacrifice that is well worth making. I think that stories of kids who were damaged by parents who stuck together for the family's sake are grossly exaggerated. They're offered as justification for their behavior by couples who split, despite the children.

Of one thing I am totally certain: neither Joan nor I could have raised our six children without each other's help. When Jody was in her early teens and she and Joan couldn't communicate without fighting, I could always make Jody smile. When Billy was in his nasty phase and snarled any time I spoke to him, it was Joan who could get him to listen. With two of us in our home one of us could always help whatever child was going through some outrageous phase. I have nothing but admiration for the parent who can single-handedly raise one or more children and do it well. They are rare and gifted people.

Let's now assume that your husband (we'll call him Ralph) has been in the throes of a mid-life crisis for eighteen months. He's staying out two nights a week, and you suspect that he's spending those two nights with a young woman about thirty years old (twenty years younger than he is), who works for the same insurance company that employs him.

You're forty-five and your daughter is ten and the two boys seventeen and nineteen. When he's home on the weekends, sometimes he'll toss a football with his sons, chat about school with his daughter, take everyone to the movies. Often, however, he prefers to sit around drinking beer and watching television. He has switched to light beer because he wants to look better in the mod clothes he just bought, and he's using Grecian Formula regularly to get the gray out of his hair. He yells every time a bill comes in for a new piece of furniture to replace some worn-out relic, and he complains because you need so much money to feed the family, even though you're a careful shopper. The only time he thinks of sex is when he's half tanked up on Saturday night and then he has difficulty getting an erection. For which, of course, he blames you.

You've spent a good part of the last eighteen months trying to help him. You've gently reminded him that he's drinking more than is good for him. You point out that his income has dropped and you wonder if he's neglecting his work. You tell him that the children think he's a grouch. When he complains about what you're spending on food you remind him that the car payments have soared since he turned the station wagon in for a sports car. You've suggested that he should see a counselor, assuring him that you'd go along too, but he says, "There's nothing wrong with me," and is angry at the very suggestion that there might be. What next?

Frankly, I think it's time to start making plans. There are the three kids to consider, of course, and the husband to whom you've been married for twenty-two years, and your parents and his parents. Have we left anyone out? Of course! How silly! We've left *you* out.

In fact, if you're like many women in their forties, you've been left out of consideration almost from the moment you said "I do." That's the way it was twenty years ago, in those dear days when, as part of the marriage vows, women promised to love, honor, and obey their husbands. (Incidentally, does anyone say those vows anymore? I've been to a lot of weddings in the last ten years and I don't recall hearing that "obey" business even once. Not that it isn't implicit, still, in some marriages.)

But there's no sense trying to turn the clock back. Now he's fifty, you're forty-five, and life has become a living hell. You've spent the last eighteen months trying to get back the husband you once had. In the mail I received from women married to men in crisis, this was the almost universal plea: "I just want my husband to get back to being the kind, loving, husband and father he once was." (I wonder how many of these men ever were as nice as their wives, looking back, seemed to think they were.) Are you going to spend another eighteen months hoping to turn things around? If he's no better after those eighteen months, will you spend another eighteen months—or maybe another two years or even three years—trying to salvage what was once a happy marriage?

That is, of course, up to you but, based on my experience with patients, and on the many discussions I've had with counselors, my advice is this: eighteen months of life with a man who is treating you like dirt is enough. It's certainly reasonable to spend eighteen months trying to hold together a marriage that was once tolerable, even pleasant. But eighteen months is enough. If things haven't improved in that time, chances are they won't improve; at least they won't improve if you keep making excuses for him. Now is the time, if you'll excuse the phrase, to kick his ass, figuratively and perhaps, if the opportunity presents itself, even literally. Now is the time, after all these years, to start putting yourself first.

EVALUATING YOURSELF

How does the women who has decided she's had enough of her mid-life-crisis husband start changing her life?

The first thing she has to do is make certain that her self-esteem is as great as it should be. It is terribly distressing to discover how little self-esteem many women have—particularly women in their forties and fifties, but even younger women. We like to think we've made a lot of progress toward sexual equality in the last twenty years, and I suppose we have; but ours is still a male-dominated society. As I have said, my wife and I have six children—three girls, three boys— and even though my three daughters all graduated from college (two from Yale, one from Tufts), and are about as liberated in their thinking as any women I know, I still worry much more about them than I do about my sons. Everything is tougher for a woman than it is for a man. Going to the movies alone; having dinner in a restaurant alone; traveling; finding a safe apartment; arranging a social life. It's still, by and large, true that the woman who doesn't marry, doesn't marry because the man or men she would have liked to marry never asked her. The man who stays single usually does so because he never found anyone he wanted to marry. (That isn't universally true, but it's close enough so as to make no difference.)

To get back to self-esteem, try this test. Ask a man who he is. He'll probably say something like, "I'm Charlie Jones. I'm forty-five years old and I'm assistant to the vice president of the Amalgamated Insurance Company. I carry a two handicap in golf and am a pretty good tennis player." Then ask Alice Jones who she is. Unfortunately she's likely to say, "I'm the wife of Charlie Jones. He's the assistant to the vice-president of Amalgamated Insurance Company. We have three children." See? Charlie tells you who he is in terms of what he does; Alice Jones tells you who she is in terms of her relationship to other people.

Admittedly, in the 1980s, many if not most women work, and they then take at least part of their identity from the jobs they hold. Although the situation is changing, in most family situations the woman's job takes second place to the man's. When a family decides to make a cross-country move because the wife has received a promotion that requires such a move and the man gives up his job to follow her, it's often worth a feature story in a local newspaper. Even national magazines have run pieces on this phenomenon. But when a woman gives up her job so she and the children can go with the man to the place his boss has transferred him, that is definitely not news. I wish it weren't true, and for women under thirty it is certainly not as true as it is for those over thirty, but many women still depend on their husbands for their identity.

For the woman whose husband is in a mid-life crisis, this dependency is frightening. If she's dependent on her husband and/or children for her identity and they leave her, she becomes, in her own eyes, nothing. Certainly, as her children grow older, they are going to leave her, in the sense that they will be off to school, involved in their own friends and activities, needing her less and less. If her husband starts staying out nights, finds a girl friend, sits and drinks and watches television in the evening, he's less dependent on her. Now, for her identity, she must depend on herself and, after a number of years of defining herself in terms of her family, that can be difficult to do.

I would have thought this problem of dependency wouldn't

be as prevalent in women in their thirties, many of whom have jobs outside their homes, but apparently it is. The idea that the woman is the mainstay of the home, the one responsible for the well-being of the family, is so thoroughly ingrained in our society that even working women have a strong tendency to define themselves in terms of family. If the family is crumbling, as it often is at crisis time, she has to learn to stand independently. She has to learn to say, and think, "I'm Alice Jones. I'm an intelligent woman who happens to be a homemaker. I know enough about economics and foreign policy to discuss these things in depth with other intelligent people. I have a husband and three children and we have had, up to now, a pleasant relationship, but if it dissolves then I, Alice Jones, will continue to thrive. I don't depend on anyone else for my existence. I can lead a full life with or without my family." Naturally, Alice Jones isn't going to shout this sort of statement to the world in general, but she ought to be able to say it to herself and mean it.

It isn't easy to do. This brings us to the matter of female support groups. The woman whose husband is going through a mid-life crisis would be well advised to join a support group of women who are in predicaments similar to hers.

Joyce Bonafield, a counselor who is very much involved in the women's movement in Minneapolis, told me, "Support groups can be invaluable for the woman whose husband is going through a mid-life crisis. Twenty-six support groups are organized by Chrysalis, which is our women's center. About one third of those groups are made up of women who are in what we call an 'uncoupling' phase. Women who have about had it with their mid-life crisis husbands will find support in one of these groups.

"That doesn't mean that the support group would persuade them to get a divorce or separation. The support group, which usually involves about eight women and certainly no more than twelve, meets once a week. The women get a chance to talk about their problems and to hear how other women have dealt with their relationships. The dialogue is given a direction by two well-trained counselors, sometimes women working for their masters or doctorate in sociology or human relations. The meetings last two hours and most women attend for eight weeks. They then skip a week and a new group starts, though some women may stay on for another series of eight weeks. Some may continue to come for a year or more, as long as they find the meetings helpful."

I had mentioned to Ms. Bonafield the problem of self-esteem. "In January of 1983, we set up a support group to help women regain self-esteem. We didn't advertise at all but, simply by word of mouth, we had a group of eight within a week. In another week we had a waiting list of another eight women—all by word of mouth. So we decided to start another group. When we continued to have women come to us, hoping to join a group, we started another waiting list, telling them that we'd work them into a group as soon as an eight-week series ended. But some of them didn't want to wait; they looked upon their self-esteem problem as an emergency. They begged us to refer them to a group somewhere else.

"But we didn't know of any other groups, so we started a third group, and we still have a waiting list; we're probably going to have to start another group. We're finding that a lot of these women feel they need more than one eight-week series of meetings.

"Frankly, we've been amazed. The problem of low self-esteem among women is much more prevalent than we originally thought. Not just women in their late forties or fifties either; women in their thirties and even their late twenties see this as a major problem, too. At the self-esteem group meetings women can talk about their insecurities, their fears, their lack of confidence. Other women will point out their strengths, tell them how they've solved similar problems.

Eventually they learn to be proud of themselves, to say, 'Hey, I'm a darn good person in my own right.' It's sad to realize how many women lack that conviction."

A support group would certainly be a big help to a woman who has been battered physically or—more commonly—psychologically, by a man in mid-life crisis, but even without one she ought to be able to recognize her own value. One simple technique I've suggested to my patients is to take a week, or preferably two, off from the home—to visit a relative if they can't afford to take a vacation. And they should not make any provisions for the family they leave behind. I've known women who, for one reason or another, have had to leave home for a week or ten days, and for the week before they leave they work twice as hard as they normally do, preparing and freezing food that can be thawed for meals in their absence, making arrangements to have the laundry done, arranging for a cleaning woman to come in every third day. I tell them that this time they ought to just pack their bags and go. Leave the family completely on its own. And if the house is a mess when they return, as it certainly will be, have two or three people come in for as long as is necessary to straighten it out and then hand the bill to their husband. That ought to boost their self-esteem.

I realize that I'm oversimplifying. If lack of self-esteem is a problem of long standing, as it seems to be with many women, then it isn't going to be eliminated in a few days. I think, however, that if a woman is aware that this is a problem, she's come at least halfway to its solution. If she just sits down and lists her positive qualities, the many things she has done for others over the years of her marriage, that should help raise her self-esteem. If that doesn't work, then in another column she should list all the things her husband has done and is doing that are driving her up the wall. With a husband in mid-life crisis, that could well be a long list, one that will make a woman proud she is who she is, and darned glad she's not he.

MAKING THE BREAK

Once you're on the way to regaining your self-esteem, the next thing you have to consider is your main problem: this man to whom you've been married, who is going through a mid-life crisis. We're assuming that you've spent the last eighteen months trying to help him, trying to persuade him that this is not the time to give up his insurance agency and become a lobster fisherman. You have also told him that if he really wants to continue his affair with the thirty-year-old he's running around with, he's going to have to move out. You've explained that the mod clothes look ridiculous on him and that, foolish as the Grecian Formula seemed, the blond toupee is even worse. You've made it very clear that the answer to all his problems does not lie at the bottom of a Jack Daniel's bottle. He has ignored all your advice, your support hasn't improved things one iota, and now you have to decide what to do next. To repeat the question I raised earlier: are you going to stick with him for another six months, or year, or more, making the best of a bad situation, or are you going to make a break?

Let me tell you right now that when you ask the wives of men in crisis that question bluntly—just as I've put it—most will immediately say, "Oh, I want to make a change. I'm ready to do anything." But when it comes to the nitty gritty, that isn't the way it works out.

Before making any sort of move you ought to look carefully at your situation from a few different points of view. The first point of view is the factual one.

What are the facts? Not just in general—"He's misbehaving"—but specifically. *How* is he misbehaving? As far as sexual infidelity is concerned, is he picking up a new woman every week or does he have an ongoing affair that shows some signs of stability? How does he feel about this woman or women? Does he tell you that he still loves you and, if so, do you believe him? You may not know the answers to all these questions, but you ought to try to get them. One good way is just to ask him.

And his drinking: exactly how bad is it? Does he get roaring drunk and drive his car into ditches, or worse? Has he had trouble with the law? Does he get belligerent? Does he ever hit you or the children? Or is he a quiet drunk, one of those people who just sit in front of the television set, drinking for hours? How much does his drinking bother you?

He talks about quitting his job, but has he done anything about it? Does he still go to work every day? Has anyone from his office told you that he's no longer doing his job properly? Is his salary the same as it has been? If he works on commission, is he earning as much as he did a year ago? Are the bills getting paid? Are you still able to buy clothes for the kids and yourself as freely as you once did? In brief, has his attitude toward his job actually affected your life-style in any way?

There are dozens of other questions you should ask and answer; the exact questions will depend on how his mid-life crisis is affecting him. Ask those questions so that you will have all the facts clear in your mind.

Once you have the facts clear, the next way you have to look at the situation is a reflective one: how do you really feel about all this? The question is not how should you feel, or how does your mother or sister think you should feel, but how do *you* feel. Some women don't really mind if their husbands have sexual relationships with other women, as long as those relations are superficial ones. Other women absolutely cannot tolerate the idea that their husband has had even casual sex with another woman. There isn't any right or wrong way to feel about your husband and extra-marital sex. How you will feel may depend on your upbringing, your religion, your own sexual desires. But if his playing around doesn't really bother you, for heaven's sake don't pretend that it does. Some women who really don't care much for sex are secretly happy when their husbands establish a sexual relationship with another woman or women. Reflect on his sexual behavior, and then be honest with yourself.

The same thing applies to his drinking. Few women will tolerate drinking if it leads to physical abuse. Some women can't stand a man who habitually sits and gets pie-eyed every evening; others like the peace and quiet his solitary drinking affords them. Don't be ashamed to admit that his boozing doesn't bother you, if that is the case.

What about his job dissatisfaction? Assuming you've talked it over and have decided that he's going to continue in the job he has, how much does his dissatisfaction bother you? If he's constantly groaning and moaning about his work, does that make you want to scream? Or can you put up with it as long as he continues to bring in a decent salary? If the latter is the case, then admit it. Your attitude is nothing to be ashamed of.

Next, consider his behavior from an interpretive point of view. What does all this mean to you? How does his playing around affect your self-esteem? Does it make you feel sexually unappealing? Or do you think that it just goes to prove that men will be men?

Is his drinking just a character weakness on his part that you hope will be temporary? Or do you interpret his drinking as a sign that he really wants to escape your company? If so, does that make you feel inadequate, even worthless? Do you dwell on this feeling or does it only rarely bother you?

Considering the male mid-life crisis from an interpretive point of view is one of the most difficult things to do. Finding

out what all this really means to you can be trying. It's sometimes hard to admit just how much his behavior really pains
you. It can be equally difficult to admit to yourself that, in
your heart of hearts, you no longer really give a damn about
his behavior; that you've lost all love and/or respect for the
man you married, who is the father of your children. Be
honest. It's difficult, but essential.

Because the final way that you have to look at your situation—after you've got the facts straight, have given it enough
thought, and have interpreted its meaning—is at the deci-
sion-making level. What are you going to do about all this?

Essentially, you have two choices: either you go on as you
are or you make radical changes. Remember, we're assuming
at this point that you've spent at least eighteen months living
with this man in crisis, working hard to help him through
it. You've done your very best to make life not only tolerable
but pleasant—even happy—for him, the children, and you.
Now you're facing up to the fact that all your efforts haven't
been successful. You've spent a lot of time reviewing the
situation and now you either act or don't act. Which will
it be?

Let me tell you that a lot of women—probably the majority—decide to act. Then, after taking the first tentative
steps—perhaps talking it over with a relative and making a
preliminary visit to a lawyer—they change their minds. Making radical changes in their lives is more than they want to
handle. So they let things go on as they are.

Most counselors believe that the women who make these
false starts do so because they haven't really looked at their
situations as closely as they should have. "Particularly from
the interpretive point of view," one very experienced counselor told me. "The woman gets the facts straight, and she
reflects on them, but she skips over the interpretive point of
view. Often she doesn't want to look at what the situation
really means to her, probably because she doesn't want to

lose the little self-esteem she has left. But it's far better to take a very close look at things before she acts. Even if she decides not to act, that's a positive step. She has made a decision. She hasn't just let things drift. In a sense she has said, 'I prefer the devil I know to the devil I don't know,' and she takes pride in having made that choice. She has assumed some mastery over her own life."

Now, however, let's assume that the woman decides to take action. She's looked closely at her life and has concluded that this man in crisis is not a person with whom she wants to spend the rest of her life. Admittedly, there's a chance that he'll change, but that chance seems increasingly remote. Even if he changes, so much damage has already been done to their relationship that she doesn't think she can ever again live happily and comfortably with him. She decides that break-up time is here. Now she has to figure out how to go about it.

CONSIDERING OPTIONS

The first step is to consider her options. These are going to vary in quality and number, depending on all sorts of factors, but one thing she is certainly going to find is that she has many more options than she thought she did. That is an almost universal truth.

Let's assume that the woman is forty-five, her husband fifty. They've been married twenty-five years and have three children—Ralph, twenty-three; Peter, nineteen; and Mary, fifteen. We'll call the wife and mother Janice, the husband Frank. If Janice is going to leave Frank, what are her options?

First, there must be a general discussion between Janice, Frank, and the children. Some of the children may be ready to go off on their own. Others may want to live with either Janice or Frank. Janice may want one or more of the children with her; on the other hand, Frank may want them with him.

Assuming Frank was a decent enough guy, at least until he went into crisis, an equitable agreement can probably be reached. If it doesn't work, it can be altered later.

One thing is certain. Once Janice is living independently of Frank, with or without one of the children, she is free to decide how to live the rest of her life. She may still be a part-time homemaker but it no longer will require all her energy and devotion. A much wider world of opportunity is now open to her.

Let's assume Janice went to college for just one year before she married Frank. She may want to go back to college and finish her education. Why not? Perhaps she'll have to go at night, if she has to support herself, but that can be managed.

How? There's no evening college in the little town where Janice lives. There's no day college either, for that matter. But who said Janice is going to continue to live in that small town? Maybe she'll want to, but perhaps she won't. Moving is one of the options now open to her; one that wasn't available when she had to live where Frank lived because of his job.

Janice, unfortunately, hasn't any job skills. Ralph was born a year after Janice married, so she's never been in the work force. She's not qualified to work.

Nonsense. Admittedly, she hasn't the experience or education that might automatically open the door to a high-level position, but even in a recession there are entry-level jobs available in many businesses for a reasonably bright woman. While she's holding down the entry-level job there's nothing to stop her from acquiring other skills, by taking night courses in a high school or vocational school. The opportunities are there for those who want to seek them out.

"But entry-level jobs are boring," someone will certainly say. "Compared to what?" I ask. If you've been a homemaker for twenty-five years, you may find that an entry-level job is a chance to get out among adults for eight hours a day, the most exciting situation you've been in in a long, long time.

One counselor I know always says to the woman who is about to leave her husband, "Shut your eyes. Now think back twenty-five years, to the time before you decided to get married. What did you want to be then?" Sometimes a woman will say "a stewardess"; sometimes "a nurse." A woman who had been ahead of her time might say "a lawyer" or "a doctor" or "a business executive," though twenty-five years ago those weren't careers many women considered.

Whatever the answer, the counselor will usually say, "Why not now?" At first the woman is usually shocked, as if the suggestion were a joke. But the more she thinks about it, the more they discuss it, the more real the possibility becomes. Sometimes the dream has to be modified; instead of becoming a registered nurse the woman will decide to become a practical nurse. Instead of becoming a lawyer, she'll elect to become a paralegal. Instead of a doctor, she'll decide to become the medical technician. The point is she'll realize that the dream she dreamt so long ago can now become a reality, or at least she can get much closer to realizing it than she thought.

It is not, of course, always necessary to even modify the dream. I know, for example, one woman of forty with four children who got divorced, worked for two years as a paralegal, and then went to law school. At forty-seven she is a very successful attorney with a large law firm, and she loves it. "That divorce was the best thing that ever happened to me," she said. "I came within inches of keeping the marriage together for the sake of the kids. That would have been the worst thing I could have done—for them, for me, and even for my former husband."

When considering her options, a woman ought to consider her family and friends. Giving up a husband doesn't necessarily mean that she's going to lose the support of his family. In fact, of all the couples I know who have parted company at crisis time, I'd estimate that in the majority of cases the wife got more support from the husband's family than the husband did. Probably, I suspect, because when a family splits during crisis time it seems apparent to almost everyone that the fault lies with the husband. I am certain that if ever Joan and I split up, crisis time or not, my mother's support would go to Joan. They are very close. It's quite common for a wife to become closer to her husband's mother than is the husband himself. (I base this on personal impressions. If there's any proof one way or the other I've been unable to find it.)

Family and friends are considered an option because they can help the woman who is in transition from married to independent status. Of course, some women are married and independent but, for many, marriage means dependence. When and if a woman considers moving she ought to weigh what she would be giving up in family support by her move. If her own family lives in some distant place, it would be worth considering that as an incentive for moving, with one big caveat. A family may welcome their married daughter and her kids for a short visit; it's quite another thing to welcome them as permanent boarders or even close neighbors. I believe that one reason I've always gotten along well with my mother is that I've lived in Minnesota for the last twenty-three years, while she continues to live in Massachusetts. If we were together too often I think she'd drive me crazy, and I know I'd drive her up a wall.

There's a rule in surgery that says, "Don't, until the last possible minute, go so far toward removing an organ that you can't possibly retain it if it proves to be necessary." For example, when I start to take out a stomach containing a bleeding ulcer, I may divide a lot of the blood vessels to the stomach early, but I always leave a few critical ones in place just in case, at the last moment, I find that the ulcer is so adherent to the pancreas or a major vein that it can't be safely removed. If I make the decision that the stomach can't be safely removed, I can do an alternative operation. I won't have harmed the stomach as long as I've left it a lesser but adequate blood supply. This is simply the surgical analogy to the old saying, "Don't burn your bridges behind you."

In splitting from your partner, the temporary separation rather than the divorce is equivalent to saving the bridge. Get a legal separation—get him out of your life for six months or even a year. If you decide after that time that, bad as life is with him, it's worse without him, you can probably get him back. Of course, you're running the risk that separation will so please him that he won't want a reunion, but that doesn't often happen. The only thing you have to be careful of, when going the separation route, is that you don't tend to think of it as a temporary measure; think of it as a preliminary step to a complete separation. Otherwise your mind set will not be such that you'll really be preparing emotionally and physically for a complete break.

One option I've already mentioned should certainly be called into play now: get in touch with a support group. If you live in a small town you may not find one locally but, believe me, even if it means a 100-mile trip twice a week, it's a trip well worth making.

Imagine what a support group can do for you. Here you are, after twenty-five years of marriage, planning to make a decision that will completely alter your life and the lives of your children and husband. All the problems are new to you; many you probably haven't even thought of. In a support group you'll find six or eight other women with problems very much like yours. Some of them will have solved some of their problems and their solutions may be ones you can use. Ideas that you have may prove helpful to them. And the counselors, who direct and structure the talk that goes on at these support sessions, have been down this road many times. Not only may they be able to help you with specific problems, but they can tell you where the resources are that you can call on for advice more sophisticated or technical than that which a support group can offer. Six or eight meetings with a support group, before taking irrevocable steps, will probably be the best investment you can make.

If you persist in your determination to leave your mid-life crisis man, you'll eventually want legal advice. Perhaps you have an attorney who is a friend and who could be comfortable helping you with the inevitable legal problems that separations and divorces entail. If you don't have such an attorney, you'll usually find, through the women's support groups, sources of proper legal advice. At Chrysalis, the comprehensive women's support center in Minneapolis, there are attorneys, two-thirds of whom are women, who come in as volunteers two nights a week to spend two hours answering specific questions from women who want legal help. Most women don't know what rights they have under the law if they decide they can no longer tolerate life with their husbands. These attorneys will answer their questions. Then, if they need more detailed help—papers filed, custody arrangements made, all those things—the lawyers who voluntarily staff women's support centers will usually agree to accept payment based on the client's ability to pay.

The attorneys who volunteer to serve at these women's support groups have their credentials carefully checked by the organization. Once they've begun working at the clinic, feedback from the women they've seen helps Chrysalis, and organizations like it, decide whether or not to keep specific attorneys on their lists. I might add that counselors, too, are also continually evaluated via feedback from women, so that if you seek support from a reputable women's support group, the chances are you're going to get the help you need.

One thing that support groups will not do—and I include counselors and lawyers as well—is to tell any individual woman exactly what she should do. That is a decision only she can make. As I've already said, many women get to the point where they want to see the lawyer and then, after one visit, they decide to continue as they are. Even that is helpful. They've looked at alternatives and made a choice. True, they've elected to remain in a situation that they find wearing and unhappy, but that's their choice. Often they're afraid of being alone. They've never had to work to earn the money that pays the rent and feeds and clothes the family. They're now afraid they are too old or too inadequate to do those things. They'll never know, now, whether they could have made it on their own, but again that's their choice. They are free agents.

But let's assume you've done all you can with your husband: you've changed yourself to meet the new standards he seems to prefer (within reason, of course; you're not going to dress like a floozy or behave like one just because that's the sort of woman he seems now to prefer) and nothing has worked. You've talked to family and friends, you've discussed the situation with your children, you've decided either to go back to school, to get a job, or to do both; or, if the kids are small and need you at home, you've found a lawyer who will see to it that your husband provides you with enough money to live on. Not luxuriously, probably, but in reasonable comfort. After the waiting period is over, the judge will grant you a divorce and you'll be free. You pick up your troubles and your husband picks up his, including all the trash he has acquired during his crisis time. How are things going to go?

HOW ARE YOU GOING TO DO WITHOUT HIM?

Things will probably go surprisingly well. That isn't universally true, of course. Some women are going to regret signing the separation or divorce papers almost from the moment that they do so. They're going to spend several days, maybe even a couple of weeks, crying because they've taken

the steps to break up their marriage. They'll feel like failures.
They may have been brought up to believe that it was the
woman's job to hold the marriage together and they've failed.
(Incidentally, whoever managed to plant the idea that the
success of a marriage was mostly dependent on the woman
must have been the biggest male chauvinistic pig in the world,
and an effective one. Even in what we consider the Enlight-
ened Eighties that idea is still imbedded in the subconscious
of many women. The fact is that the success of a marriage
depends equally on both parties.)

I believe, generally speaking, that the woman who works
hard, for anywhere from six months to two years, trying to
get a mid-life crisis husband to return to a life-style that is
tolerable for him, her, and the children, is better off to call
it quits when that time is up. She doesn't have to rush into
a divorce, though that may be a reasonable option, but after
six months or two years of hell she deserves a break—a separation at the very least. If she can only find the courage to
make that break—and it's admittedly not easy to do—I think
she's probably going to find that life without him is much
more pleasant than it has been with him. I think, after two
or three weeks, she's going to be asking herself, "Why didn't
I do this three months ago?" Some of the happiest women
I've met are women who parted from mid-life crisis husbands
after a year or two of sheer misery. After reading my mail
and talking to women who made the break, and others who
didn't, I think—though there are exceptions on both sides—
the evidence is fairly persuasive that those that made the
break are happier.

To put this in proper perspective let me make it very clear:
a mid-life crisis is often a temporary affair. Like most crises
it will eventually come to an end, in which case the participants can go on *almost* as before. My contention is that a
mid-life crisis that lasts more than two years, despite good-
will efforts by both parties to resolve it, is best terminated

by separation. The woman, almost certainly, will find her new status a joy. This may or may not prove to be true for the man.

I have evidence to offer that in many cases I'm correct in making such a strong statement.

As I've already mentioned, when I wrote an article on the mid-life crisis in 1981, I received more mail and phone calls than I had from any other article I'd ever written. I answered most of these women (and a few men), but really didn't have any practical advice to offer. However, I kept their letters and when I decided to write this book I phoned to find out what had happened to them in the three years since they had written to me. I've changed names and some identifying characteristics; otherwise, these are their stories as they told them to me.

Jane Sullivan was fifty-one, her husband, Ray, was fifty-five when she wrote to me. "At that time," she told me when I called, "he had just gone off to California with a twenty-seven-year-old divorcée with a two-year-old child. He left me behind in Ohio with our son, twenty-three, and our two daughters, sixteen and fifteen. We had been married twenty-six years, had always gotten along well together, and I had worked with him to build an engineering company that had been quite successful. I studied architecture in college and I had made a significant contribution to our business.

"What precipitated his crisis, I think, was the economy. At that time a lot of businesses, including ours, were in a slump. He decided to take what he considered an easy out: leave me and the children behind and run off. He'd had other symptoms of the mid-life crisis before he left: he'd been drinking too much; had been staying out late at night; had been ignoring the kids. I suspected that he'd found a girl friend, but our sex life had continued to be active, so I wasn't sure until he actually made the break.

"When he left, leaving me a note, I called the three kids

together and told them exactly what had happened. It was funny; they all reacted differently. Our son said, 'Heck, he doesn't even know her. How dumb can he be?' My sixteen-year-old daughter was devastated. She cried for two days. I guess she was hurt more than anything. The fifteen-year-old was just plain mad.

"I kept working; the business was in both of our names and I wanted to hold it together. I was hurt, of course, but I was angry, too. Angry or not, though, if he wanted to run off with another woman, I couldn't stop him. But I'm a self-confident person and I thought I could survive.

"Six weeks after Ray left, I got a call from California. He told me he knew now that he'd made a mistake and so did his girl friend. She'd been looking for security for herself and her child, he'd been looking for some young, sexy companionship, and when they had it they both realized the price was too high. They were already bored with each other. He wanted to come home; I told him I'd think about it and put it to a vote.

"Two days later he called me back. I told him the vote was three to one against. I wouldn't tell him who voted which way. We were hanging on and I didn't want him to come back just to run off again. Besides, I have to admit that I was beginning to enjoy my independence. I'd found out I could get by quite nicely without him.

"He called every week or so for the next six months. He had a job with an engineering firm and was sending money home. His girl friend had packed up and left. After six months I decided to take the two girls and fly to California for a week. We stayed in a motel near where he lived and I saw Ray most days and every evening. It was just like our courting days all over again and, to tell you the truth, I loved it. It's funny how, once you're married, the courting immediately stops. I hadn't realized how much I missed it.

"We also talked—more in that week than we had in twenty

years. About our lives together, the children, how we really felt about each other and what we were doing. What a shame that people stop talking almost as soon as they're married.

"After the week in California, I went home. I told him I wanted to think about it all away from him, but when he called a week later I said 'Come on home. The vote is now four to zero in your favor.' So he came back.

"Things are fine now, but they aren't quite the same as they were before he left. Ray's still a workaholic—I don't think that will ever change—but he does take time off to visit with the kids and do things with them. Our son is now an engineer, too, and he and his dad find plenty to talk about.

"I'm nowhere near as dependent on him as I once was. There's a college in a city sixty miles from where we live, and two nights a week I go there and take courses. I have a small one-bedroom apartment there, and I often stay overnight. The kids are quite grown up—the youngest is eighteen now—and Ray takes responsibility for them when I'm away.

"Our sex life is fine again, but I have to admit that his affair still bothers me. If I met a man I admired, and could do so discreetly, I'm not certain I wouldn't have an affair. That's probably a childish reaction, and I suppose I'll get over it, but at the moment that's how I feel.

"My biggest regret is all those years when we weren't really communicating. I think the male mid-life crisis is a chemical thing; something just goes wrong in the nervous system. But I also think that if a husband and wife are really communicating, foolish, painful episodes can be averted.

"My second biggest regret is that I didn't discover until I was fifty-one that I could get along just fine on my own. I was never a clinging vine—I can see where that sort of wife would drive a man crazy—but I wasn't as independent as I should have been. If I was going to work I should have worked for another engineering company, not his.

"Anyway, now that he's back and it's over, I think I'm a

stronger person, our marriage is better, and our kids have seen what can happen if they don't nurture their marriages. We all learned from it."

Alice Tatro was forty-two, her husband, Jack, forty-five, when she wrote to me. They had four children—two girls twenty and sixteen, two boys eighteen and fourteen. Her husband was a foreman in a plant that builds heavy equipment. In her letter she said, "My husband has been going through this crisis for three years now, and I'd like to know how long it can possibly last. You gave advice to him, but not to the wife who has to cope. I've been hanging in there for three years and now, frankly, I'm tired of hanging. We've been to marriage counselors, but he just won't reveal much of himself. I feel that our four children are suffering as much as we are, and some solution must be worked out." She ended her letter by saying that she had decided to give the marriage two more months and if things weren't better she'd separate. She hoped I could help her. I suggested some books she could read, but otherwise had no specific advice to give.

In her letter Ms. Tatro had mentioned those things typical of a crisis. Her husband was drinking far too much, staying out all night at least twice a week, ignoring his children. He had traded in his Chevette for a convertible, let his hair grow, and had had it styled in a mod cut. She wasn't sure he was playing around but suspected that was the case.

When I phoned Ms. Tatro she was most cooperative. "I appreciated your letter," she said, "and I read the books you mentioned, but they didn't help much. When the two months were up I told him I couldn't take it any longer, that he wasn't much of a father to the kids anyway, and that I wanted a separation. He said he was sorry but didn't seem able to help himself, and he left.

"That was three years ago. I went to a lawyer and he arranged to get support money for me and the children; at that time I felt I ought to be home with the children as much as I could. I did start taking night courses, though, learning typing and enough about computers to get a secretarial job. I had never had any college. It was tough for the first year. I had really loved Jack and he'd been a good husband for eighteen of our twenty-one years together. But even though I missed him sometimes, all I had to do was think of how miserable those last three years had been and I was glad he was gone. When he'd come over to see the children I'd talk to him for a few minutes, but then I'd go off to see my mother. I was lucky in having both my mother and a younger sister living near by.

"Last year my older daughter got married—after finishing college, I'm happy to say—and since our youngest was sixteen I felt I could take a full-time job. In fact, I'm very proud of myself. I started as a secretary in a very big insurance firm near where I live and I've just been promoted to office manager. I don't take any more support money from Jack, though he does help with the children, and I'm very self-sufficient. You can't believe how wonderful it feels to discover you can stand on your own two feet.

"Jack stops by once in a while to see our children. He seems to have gotten over whatever it was that was bothering him for those three years. His hair looks like the hair of a forty-eight-year-old man should look, and I've heard from mutual friends that he's not drinking much anymore.

"Last month he asked me if I'd like to go out to dinner; I'm taking a lot better care of myself since I went to work and if I do say so I look pretty attractive for a woman of forty-five. I told him 'No thanks' as gently as I could. It's funny, but as far as I'm concerned there's just no spark between us anymore. I think those three awful years killed it.

"But that doesn't mean I'm planning to spend the rest of my life alone. I've had a lot of dates over the last six months (it's amazing how many divorced men there are out there) and there's one fellow—one of our agents, in fact—whom I've been dating quite regularly. He likes movies, as I do—Jack would never go—and he also likes jazz, which I've always enjoyed. I'm not rushing into anything, but who knows what may happen?

"The kids are doing fine. They still love their dad, but they've never wanted to go and live with him. I think those three years damaged their relationship with their father. I tried to keep our fights to ourselves, but kids don't miss much.

"I'm sorry it all happened, but it seems to be working out pretty well. In a way, maybe it was a good thing—at least for me. To tell you the truth, I'm about as happy now as I've ever been."

Lorraine Stephens's husband, Bruce, had "gone whacky right after his fiftieth birthday," she wrote me. "That birthday seemed to do something to him; it was just as if someone had thrown a switch. One week he was a nice, easy-going, loving husband, to whom I'd been married for thirty years; the next he was a crazy man who got drunk all the time, ignored the children, said nasty things to me. It was like Dr. Jekyll and Mr. Hyde." I had written an unhelpful note, but when I called she was happy to bring me up-to-date.

"We live in a nice quiet town in Pennsylvania, right in the heart of the steel country. He'd been a salesman, and a good one, for twenty-eight years. The firm he worked for was very conservative; they didn't like loud-mouthed, flamboyant people. We had three children, two boys twenty-eight and twenty-six and a daughter twenty-four. We were big on family picnics, walks in the woods, fishing, and gardening. He was the kind of man who was always puttering around, fixing up the house. We also had a great sex life; nothing kinky, but plenty active.

"Right after his fiftieth birthday he met a salesman from

a different company who told Bruce that he was missing a lot of fun. This man was on the road a lot—Bruce had only rarely had to stay away from home—and he thought that was great. Swinging parties all the time, lots of drinking, girls in every town. Anyway, Bruce switched companies.

"He didn't travel much, but now it was party, party all the time. Lots of drinking, late nights, weekends of golf and more parties. Everything went on an expense account. No more walks in the country, no more picnics, no more playing catch with the boys. He turned into a swinger. He even bought a red sports car.

"Honestly, Dr. Nolen, I thought he might have a brain tumor—that's how much he changed. I got him to go to a doctor, but the doctor said he was healthy. I couldn't take it. I refused to go to his parties. Then he started tearing into me, putting me down in front of the children. He tried to make a nothing out of me. I had loved him; now I didn't even like him.

"I got him to go to another doctor. When he came home from that visit, do you know what he said to me? 'Guess what we talked about? Liz.' Liz was the name of his girl friend at that time. Oh, but he was cruel.

"He went to another doctor. In fact, by the time we were through he'd been to four doctors, three ministers, and one psychologist. This doctor told him to make out a list of things he didn't like about me. He made a list of twenty-six things! Can you imagine? Where had these things been all our lives? He even had things like 'puts my coffee cup in wrong place' on his list.

"I took the list, read it, and one by one I changed all twenty-six things. When it was done I said to him, 'All right, this is it. I've changed everything you wanted changed. I'm not changing anymore. If you don't like the way I am now, then it's over.'

"My mother, my sister, my brother, and all our friends

had been telling me for two years that I ought to leave him. I stuck by him because we'd had thirty good years together. I didn't want to throw those away. But now I'd had it. I couldn't take any more. I told him, 'You can't work for that company and live with me.'

"You know what happened? Almost as suddenly as he'd gone crazy, he changed back again. He quit the company he had joined and went back to his old job. He'd made more money with his new job, but he'd spent it all on clothes anyway, so the lower salary didn't matter. He stopped the drinking and the running around. He got back to talking with the kids. I don't know if it was because I finally threatened to walk out or if he was just getting over whatever it was that caused him to go berserk, but he changed back to the man I had loved.

"Now we take walks and go on picnics like we used to. He ushers at church again and he had a great garden this year. Our sex life, which had gone to pieces, is back to what I'd call fine.

"I have to say though that forgiving is one thing—I've done that—but forgetting is another. He says now that he doesn't even remember some of the things he said when he was drinking, but I remember them. He may have forgotten about Liz, but I can't. Things will never be quite the same between us.

"Still, I'm glad I stuck it out. Those were two terrible years, but we'd had thirty good ones and now we hope to have more. Two of our children are married now and we have two grandchildren. I'd say life is pretty darn good. If I were advising a woman whose husband was going crazy I'd tell her to stick with him. At least it worked out well for me."

When I first heard from Rita she was thirty-eight. "My husband, Mark, just turned forty," she wrote. "We have three children, a boy fifteen and twins—a boy and a girl—ten.

Mark sells insurance but lately he's been saying he's sick of his job. He doesn't have time to enjoy all the things we've bought: cars, a boat, a lake cabin, an airplane. When he gets down, which is pretty often now, he drinks too much; but that doesn't make him better, it makes him worse. He complains because we don't have any privacy because of the kids. He's always tired, but still he pushes himself. He can't seem to sit still.

"He's involved with a woman ten years younger than himself. She's been divorced twice and has two children, one by each husband. Mark had been seeing her for a year before I found out, but I've known for ten months now and he's still carrying on. He tells me that he wants to break things off with her, but he can't seem to do it. She calls him and he lacks the willpower to resist her advances.

"I love my husband very much. I can forgive him and I don't want a divorce. I'm being as patient and understanding as I possibly can. My friends tell me I'm foolish for putting up with him but I can't give up on him when he's so confused and unhappy. He's been to a psychologist, but only once. I guess my question to you is, is there any help you can suggest?"

After hearing from Rita, I had written suggesting only that they both seek counseling. As I've said, I really didn't have any answers. Two and a half years after her original letter, I called Rita to find out what had happened.

"Not much, really," she said.

"We're not divorced. We still live together. He's still unhappy with the insurance business, but he can't seem to get out.

"He still has his girl friend. In fact, in May of this year, just five months ago, she had Mark's baby. He supports the baby, I guess; I don't know how much he gives her because he manages our finances."

"Are you happy?" I asked.

"Not really," Rita said. "Sometimes things are worse than at other times, but I'm never really happy. But I won't divorce him and his girl friend won't give him up. When she's with him she leaves things in the car so that I'll find them. I think she wants me to divorce him because then she thinks he'll go to her. She's got those three kids, and she's only thirty-two, and she wants a man in the house. But I want him here with me and our kids."

"How do your children feel about all this?" I asked.

"We never talk about it," Rita said. "I suppose they know—they'd have to be blind not to—but they don't say anything."

"Have you any plans," I asked, "any sort of deadline when you're going to do something?"

"No," she said. "I think it's the nature of men to run around. I've been living with this for four years now, and I can keep on living with it. I haven't got any education; I've never held a job. I have three kids. What else can I do?"

I suggested that she seek out a women's support group, talk to her doctor or her minister, or visit a counselor, but Rita said, "No. I've considered those things, but what good would they do? All they'd do is tell me to give him up, like my friends have been telling me for years, and I'm not going to do it. Let her give him up. He's my husband."

When Helen wrote to me she was fifty and Ted, her husband, was fifty-five.

"I've been through a living hell for the last three years," she wrote. "It all started with constant drinking, getting drunk. Then lies and cheating with women. He stayed out until 4:00 A.M. or even 7:00 A.M. six nights a week. He was a construction worker but he got early retirement because of back problems that required three operations. He was just hanging around with nothing to do.

"Our two children, a boy and a girl, were twenty-seven and thirty then. He met a woman in a bar, the same age as his daughter, and he took up with her. He swore at me, wouldn't give me money to run the house, blamed everything—his back, his drinking, everything—on me. He finally moved out of our home and in with her. He bought a four-speed, stick-shift car. He dyed his hair. His appearance is now dirty and untidy. When we were together he was always neat and clean. He has no friends because of what he has done to his family. I might add he has always hated the kind of man I've described to you.

"We were married thirty-two years when all this started. He became a stranger before my very eyes and I couldn't do anything to help him. Because he said there wasn't anything wrong with him. He brought his girl friend here and they laughed in my face. I must have cried a million tears trying to help him.

"His drinking scares me. I've talked to the police about things and they only say be careful wherever you go. My lawyer says the same thing.

"I could go on and on but I think you get the picture. I feel like I'm the other woman, the abused one. Just thought you would like to hear a wife's side of this [the male mid-life crisis].

"I do hope you will answer my letter if only to let me know you received it. Thanks."

A little over two years later, Helen told me that she and Ted were still separated, but not divorced. "He left his girl friend, or she left him six months ago," Helen said. "He lives with friends now. Our separation is legal."

"I'm very close to his mother and his brother. They can't understand what happened to him either. We'd had thirty-two good years before he went crazy. He's not drinking as much now that he's left his girl friend. He still sends me money to run the house. I've got a part-time job in a factory, so I get by. Neither our son or daughter will speak to their father. They don't even want to see him.

"What hurt so much was the way he showed off his girl friend. I would have thought he'd have the decency to keep his affair quiet. He behaved as if there weren't any rules he had to follow.

"If someone had told me ten years ago that I'd go through three years of hell when I was fifty I would have said they were crazy. The best thing that could have happened to me was his moving out. When he lived with me and drank and ran around, I didn't think I'd survive. When he left it was as if a big burden was lifted off of me.

"I don't hate him now, though I guess I did for a while. I'm just sorry for him. But I don't want him back. Not after the way he treated me. I'm a lot better off living alone. My daughter is an R.N., and she comes to visit often. She doesn't understand what got into Ted either. It was as if he had gone crazy."

When Ellen wrote to me she was thirty-nine. Her husband, Mike, was forty-four.

"Mike was never the best husband," she wrote, "but I always thought he loved me and the kids. We had five children in two and a half years (two sets of twins) and another a year and a half after that. Six beautiful, well-mannered, normal children, three girls and three boys. After much struggling he made it in his field, computer programming.

"He then turned forty. He started staying out three nights instead of his usual one. He got a curly permanent, a small car, and a pair of faded jeans. After staying out all one night he came in and said that someone at work had looked at him funny and he was going to quit his job. He did that day. A month later he left me and moved 125 miles away to his sisters' home. He rarely calls or sees those six beautiful children.

"He feels no obligation to support those children. I am

running a small stationery store we started together. Our home is being repossessed because I could not continue the house payments of $458 per month. I am still paying the medical bills he created while he was trying to figure out what was wrong.

"Our doctor does not believe in male mid-life crises. I don't have the money for a legal separation or divorce. I'm too busy trying to feed, clothe, and shelter six children to worry about it now. He has a young girl friend and no responsibilities."

Two and a half years after I received her letter I phoned Ellen. She was at work; she is a secretary-bookkeeper in an accounting firm. "Six months after I wrote you," she said, "we got a divorce.

"I'm forty-one now, he's forty-six. About the time we got a divorce he lost his job as a systems analyst, so he couldn't send me support money even if he wanted to. I got this job and I managed. The kids are just wonderful. I thank God for them. I've never had any problems with drugs or drinking or anything else. All the kids except the youngest have after-school jobs. They range from thirteen to seventeen now. Mike is working now, so he does send child support money.

"The divorce was his idea, not mine. I never really believed in divorce. I hate to admit it, but I actually begged him to stay, even though I knew he was running around. I said I'd change, if he'd only tell me how he wanted me to change. The funny thing is, he didn't know what he wanted changed. I finally said, 'Okay, if you're going to go, go.' Now I'm glad I did.

"I can't say I like being single, but I certainly wouldn't want him back. I didn't know until he was gone how moody he was. I didn't realize how tense I'd get, wondering how he'd be when he came home from work. I'm glad that's over.

"What I resent most about him is the fact that he treated

the kids so shabbily. They deserve to have a loving, caring father around while they're growing up, and they don't."

"Do you have a boy friend?" I asked.

"Not now," she said, laughing. (Ellen is a very cheerful woman. I could tell, just from talking with her on the phone, that she was a naturally good-natured person.) "I didn't go out with anyone for the first year after we were divorced. Then I decided it was time to get on with my life, so I've had dates. No one special just now."

"Are you still glad he's gone?" I asked.

She paused for a minute before answering. "I guess I can honestly say I am," she said. "I've told you about his moods, but it's more than that. I enjoy my job, and I'm good at it. I've got a lot of energy and I've started filling in my life with things he wouldn't allow me to do."

"Like what?" I asked.

"An art appreciation course," Ellen said. "I enjoy art. Swimming lessons; I didn't learn to swim when I was a kid. Amateur theater; I work at set designing. I enjoy it. In fact, I even teach a course in doll making. And I took a first-aid course this summer. I think I can say I'm quite satisfied with my life now. I did everything I could to help him through what I suppose was his mid-life crisis, but it wasn't enough. I worked at helping him for almost three years. That was long enough."

"How's he doing?" I asked.

"I don't know for sure," she said. "Whenever he comes to pick up one of the kids he has a girl friend with him, so I make a point of not being around. I wish he wouldn't bring a girl friend; not because I mind, but because I know the kids resent it. Maybe he's happy. I hope so. But I think he's going to realize later how sad it was for him not to have seen more of the kids.

"But I can't worry about him," she said with a little laugh. "I've got too much else to do."

*   *   *

What can we learn from the stories of these women?

First, it's apparent that there isn't a simple answer that is right for everyone. For one woman, a temporary separation gave her a new perspective on her own strength, and though eventually she and her husband got back together, her position in the family was no longer a subordinate one. She was just as clever and strong as her husband—possibly cleverer and stronger—and they both knew it. For her, the separation had been positive.

The women who said a permanent goodbye to their husbands were also free of regrets. They were happier than they had been in years. One of them hadn't asked for the divorce, but when it was thrust upon her she found it was a blessing she hadn't anticipated. In fact, the message that rings loudest and clearest from these stories, and dozens of others in my files, is that in no instance, when a male mid-life crisis leads to a marriage dissolution, is the woman any less happy than she was when the marriage was intact. Women learn, when the male in crisis leaves, that they can "make it" on their own. It's a rejuvenating experience.

What is to be said of the woman who clings to her husband despite the fact that for several years he had been demeaning her, even to the extent of fathering a child by another woman? At this point, all one could do is say, "I'm sorry for her." It would certainly seem that she would be much better off to leave this man, but she has been told that dozens of times and refuses to do so. She may well be afraid. She has been dependent on her husband for so long—not only for food and shelter but for identity—that she simply cannot face what she perceives as the dangers of standing on her own. So she goes on living in a world that few of us would accept. That is certainly her privilege, but once she has chosen it, it is probably futile to spend time worrying about her.

Let me emphasize again that all the women who gave up

on their husbands in crisis survived very nicely. Men should consider the implications very seriously. The message, as I see it, is that there's only so much time for a man in crisis to get his act together and get it on the road; otherwise the person whom he has depended on to be his manager, arranger, producer, and co-star may go solo. If she does, she'll be a success.

EIGHT

Last Words

HOW WILL THE MAN IN CRISIS MANAGE WITHOUT BEING MARRIED?

The man whose mid-life crisis leads to dissolution of his marriage may survive it very nicely. The odds are against it, but it happens.

Consider Al. At fifty-two, when his wife, Judy, was forty-five, Al decided he wanted to get out of the advertising business and try teaching English literature. "I'd spent most of my spare time reading for the twenty-five years I'd been in advertising, and I'd kept up with what was being published in the 'little' journals as well as in the mass-circulation magazines. My degree was in English literature. The only reason I'd gone into advertising in the first place was the money. As you know, it's hard to make much money as a teacher.

"But now the last of our three kids was about to graduate from college. I was earning $65,000 a year plus bonuses, and we had the house, the pool, the Mercedes, the whole bit— but I wasn't happy. I could no longer persuade myself that it made any difference whether a customer bought one deodorant or another; it seemed to me that I was wasting my life on a job without any real meaning.

"I talked it over with Judy and found she didn't like the idea one bit. She enjoyed our life. She liked belonging to the club, liked the big house, enjoyed the trips to Bermuda. 'We've worked hard to get where we are,' she said. 'I don't want to go back to a tiny apartment and casserole dinners.'

"She had a point. After all, we'd been together for twenty-five years and she did have a right to enjoy what she saw as the benefits of my career. I stuck with advertising, but it didn't get any better. I was bored out of my mind. I started drinking—taking a nip or two even at the office—and I could tell my boss was worried about me. Judy went her way, socially, and I went mine. She went off to play tennis doubles with her friends in the afternoon and she never wanted to miss a party. I started staying home. She got used to going alone and, to tell you the truth, I think she preferred not having me there. I was never much fun at a party.

"Six months after I'd first brought it up I decided that, whatever the price, I just couldn't go on as I was going. Judy still wouldn't go along. I told her I was sorry, but if I had to choose between her and a new career I'd have to take the new career. I felt I still loved her, but not enough to let the advertising business kill me. We had some bitter fights, but I stuck by my guns. Thank God the kids were grown up enough so that they didn't turn against either of us. They understood we'd just come to a parting of the ways.

"That was almost three years ago. Judy's lawyer took me for plenty, but I could hardly protest; I was the one who wanted out. She's still got the house and the pool and still goes to the parties. I had enough money in the agency's retirement program so that she could continue to live as we had. I heard just last week that she's about to marry a widower with a lot of dough who is very active in the club's tennis program.

"My first job after leaving the agency was teaching English at a private prep school; I didn't have the teaching credits for the public-school system. The cut in pay hurt. I dropped from over $60,000 a year to $20,000, but the gratification I got from teaching those kids more than made up for it. I took night courses at the State University and got my master's degree this June. I'm prouder of that than I am of the best ad campaign I ever put together. The three kids came to my graduation and took me out for a spaghetti dinner afterward.

"I was going to try for a college-level job, but now I'm not so sure. I like teaching high-school students. Sure, a lot of them are just interested in killing time, but when I can make Shakespeare or Milton or Updike interesting to them, it's wonderful to watch the way they catch fire. I wouldn't trade that experience for a salary three times as great.

"I don't know if I'll marry again. I have a couple of women friends whose tastes run to things like foreign movies, museums, and politics—things Joyce didn't care about. I like spending time with them, but marry one of them? I just don't know. Not for a while, certainly.

"I guess what I went through was a mid-life crisis, and I'm sorry it brought a marriage of twenty-five years to an end, but I think the split was good for both Joyce and me."

For some men the mid-life crisis had all the characteristics of an acute infectious disease.

Consider David. His mid-life crisis ran, by his own admission, the way he wanted it to run—or thought he wanted it to run.

"Frankly, Bill," he told me, "I just got tired of everything— wife, kids, job, the whole business. I was forty-five and I had plenty of money: my father had left me one bank and I had bought two others ten years earlier that were really booming. The banks ran themselves; I'd hired good people and if I stopped in at each one once a month I could keep on top of things. Two of the kids were in college and the other two were in high school, so they all had their own interests. Nancy had opened a ceramics art shop and that, together with her tennis activities, kept her busy. I felt completely unnecessary.

"I started screwing around. I'd stay in Minneapolis a couple of nights a week—'on business,' as I'd tell Nancy—and it wasn't difficult at all to find someone attractive to share my bed. I knew other guys in the same situation I was in— they owned businesses that ran themselves—and we'd get together and party three or four times a week. Sometimes we'd just drive out to the airport, catch a plane to Vegas, and spend three or four days gambling, screwing, and drinking. Back to work for a day or two, and then off again to the races.

"Sometimes, to tell you the truth, I felt as if I were on fire, just as if I had a fever. I didn't really feel like raising hell, but I did anyway. There was nothing else to do."

"Didn't you talk with Nancy about how you felt?" I asked.

"How could I?" David asked. "She was always busy with ceramics or tennis or the kids. She didn't have time to talk. The one time I did get to speak with her, one Sunday morning, she seemed to think it was all a joke. 'How can you have any problems?' she said. 'You've got plenty of money and plenty of free time. What more can you want?'

"The heck of it was, I didn't know what I wanted. After a year of hell raising I was bored with that, too. Nothing interested me. In fact, I got kind of desperate. I didn't know what to do with myself. Here I was, a guy who seemed to have the world by the tail, and deep down inside I was miserable."

"What happened?" I asked.

David smiled. "Lois happened," he said. "One night I went to a party that I thought was going to be the usual drink, eat, dance, pair-off affair. In fact, it turned out to be a benefit for the muscular dystrophy program. Lois was the chairwoman of the thing and she'd lined up a couple of doctors and a social worker who talked about what was happening as far as research was concerned. Lois was not only attractive but very intelligent and, though she had a good sense of humor, she had a serious side, too. She was a psychologist with a private practice but had a nephew with muscular dystrophy and that's what got her interested in the program.

"To make this short, I asked her out and she said yes. But when she found out the kind of life I was living she dropped me. 'Too many important things that need doing,' she said. 'You're a nice guy, but not the kind for me. Find some play-girl.'

"So we talked, and she made me see my life as she saw it. I decided I was living as I was simply because it seemed like it should be fun. She got me interested in other things— particularly in inner-city renovation—and I found that the banking knowledge I had made me a very effective advocate of some badly needed reform. I'm on half a dozen committees that are trying to arrange financing for housing projects for the poor and I spend a lot of hours every week harassing the mayor and the city council to get the legal changes we need. In fact, I'm so busy I haven't had time to go to Vegas in six months and, to be honest, I don't miss it."

"How does Nancy feel about all this?"

"That's the only sad part of it, Bill; Nancy thinks I'm nuts. She can't see why I'm willing to work for nothing for people I don't even know. She's actually angry; thinks I could earn enough to buy another bank if I worked at it. Maybe she's right, but I don't need another bank and these people do need affordable homes.

"My guess is that Nancy and I have about had it. She's not going to change and neither am I. If I'd kept going the way I was I'd have burned myself out in two years. Now I feel like a guy with a purpose—raring to go, the way I was twenty years ago. Nancy won't listen, but Lois will. I'm in love with Lois. I think we'll work it out." David seems happy to me and I suspect that he and Lois *will* work it out.

Let me make it clear that these two men are exceptions. The fact is that the majority of men whose crises lead to radical changes later regret those changes.

Leo, for example, whose wife, Marie, left him when, after two years, he was still drinking and running around with a girl half his age. "I could kick myself now," Leo told me. "I married Stephanie [his young girl friend] and it lasted exactly one year. I got tired of smoking pot and listening to punk music. I like jazz, dammit. And whenever I'd try to read a book she'd say, 'Oh, stop being such a bore.' I just couldn't take it.

"Now I'm busting my butt providing a home for Marie and the kids and an apartment for myself. I see the kids on weekends, only now that they're in their teens they don't want to leave their friends to visit their old man, and I don't blame them. I behaved like a fool. I admit it now, but Marie won't take me back. She says two years of misery was enough. She doesn't want any more. Can't say I blame her."

Paul, at forty-five, left his wife and children and sold his half interest in a very successful poultry processing business to his brother. He then went on a world tour with his new twenty-five-year-old girl friend. When they returned he opened an art gallery, which his young friend ran. The business went under in less than two years. Now Paul is a permanent fixture at the Elks Club. "What else is there to do?" he asked me. "At least here I can find someone to talk to and maybe get into a game of cards. Sure, I have a date every now and then, but at fifty I'm too old for romance. I'll never understand why I did what I did. I'd give anything to be back in the poultry business with my brother. And back with Peg and the kids as well."

*   *   *

Jim is an alcoholic. He lost his job with the engineering firm he'd been with for twenty-five years. His retirement pay goes for his apartment and booze. "I try to send Janice money for the kids' education," he says, "but there's never much to send. I don't know where it goes.

"No—that's a lie. I do know where it goes. On this stuff," he said, pointing to a highball. "Can't seem to stop, even though I know I should. Tried A.A. three times, but I can't seem to make it. I might, if I hadn't split with Janice—she'd have helped me—but it's too late now. I wouldn't listen to her for three years, and she doesn't want to try anymore."

So it goes. Male mid-life crises that lead to marriage dissolutions seem to leave the men worse off than the women. Which, I suppose, is understandable; it's only logical that he be the one whose physical and psychological being crumbles when he doesn't make it through the crisis.

HOW WILL IT ALL END?

Which brings us, finally, to roundup time. What are we to conclude about this phenomenon we call the male mid-life crisis?

First, we should again emphasize that it is, in most instances, a temporary phenomenon. The man goes into crisis. He develops the signs and symptoms we've discussed. He and his wife, with or without the assistance of others, make appropriate adjustments over the next six months to two years. Then, life goes on, not exactly as before but without radical changes. For somewhere between 70 and 80 percent of males, this is the way the crisis ends.

For the remaining 20 to 30 percent, the mid-life crisis does prompt radical changes. Whether these changes will include dissolution of the marriage (if he is married) depends on the variables we've already discussed in depth. If the marriage does dissolve because of pressures of the crisis, the woman is almost certainly going to find herself happier than she was with the man in crisis, and she may even be happier than she was with her husband before he went into crisis. I am certainly not recommending that any woman regard a male mid-life crisis as an opportunity to find a more happy life. I'm just saying that experience proves that it may turn out to be just that.

As for the man in crisis, he deserves all the help and support he can find. He is restless, unhappy, frustrated, frightened. But he must realize that, despite the support he may or may not get, it is primarily he who has to fight through this condition. After six months at the least, and two years at the most, he is going to find that his support will vanish. Initially the reaction to his crisis will be, "Poor Tom, let's do all we can to help him." Later it's going to be, "Is Tom still chasing girls, getting drunk, and moaning about his job? What kind of a boring idiot is he, anyway? Someone should tell him it's time to get off his duff, pull himself together, and get to work." The object of pity becomes one of scorn. No one can milk kindness from a mid-life crisis indefinitely.

The male mid-life crisis is a time of trial that every male experiences and into which are dragged all those closest to him. Properly managed it can end with little or no damage done; it may even end with his life and/or marriage richer than ever. Badly managed, it can lead to disastrous results, particularly for the man, but he may unwillingly hurt his wife, children, and close friends as well.

The man who decides that his mid-life crisis is a license to behave any way he wishes indefinitely, regardless of the damage it does to his loved ones, has only himself to blame for the misery that his behavior will eventually and inevitably bring him. I missed deserving that retribution by the narrowest of margins, thanks to a very wise and loving wife. I'm eternally grateful to her.